T0103679

# PRACTICING PRESENCE

## THEORY AND PRACTICE OF PASTORAL CARE

### ROB O'LYNN

WESTBOW°
PRESS
A DIVISION OF THOMAS NELSON
& ZONDERVAN

Copyright © 2014 Rob O'Lynn.

All rights reserved. No part of this book may be used or reproduced by any means, graphic, electronic, or mechanical, including photocopying, recording, taping or by any information storage retrieval system without the written permission of the publisher except in the case of brief quotations embodied in critical articles and reviews.

WestBow Press books may be ordered through booksellers or by contacting:

WestBow Press
A Division of Thomas Nelson & Zondervan
1663 Liberty Drive
Bloomington, IN 47403
www.westbowpress.com
1 (866) 928-1240

Because of the dynamic nature of the Internet, any web addresses or links contained in this book may have changed since publication and may no longer be valid. The views expressed in this work are solely those of the author and do not necessarily reflect the views of the publisher, and the publisher hereby disclaims any responsibility for them.

Any people depicted in stock imagery provided by Thinkstock are models, and such images are being used for illustrative purposes only.
Certain stock imagery © Thinkstock.

ISBN: 978-1-4908-6319-1 (sc)
ISBN: 978-1-4908-6320-7 (e)

Library of Congress Control Number: 2014922053

Printed in the United States of America.

WestBow Press rev. date: 2/2/2015

# CONTENTS

# ACKNOWLEDGEMENTS

This book would not have been possible without the influence and assistance of several individuals. First, in terms of assistance, I would like to thank my long-time research assistant Alathia "Alli" Dawn Starr for her careful reading and rereading of each stage of this manuscript. I would also like to thank my wonderful team at WestBow Press for guiding me through the publishing process. From beginning to end, their coaching and encouragement helped finally get this book into your hands. Lastly, I would like to thank my family who went numerous nights and weekends without their father while I was covering the hospital and who have waited and now again wait up until I get home from making those late night hospital and home visits to church members.

Second, in terms of influence, I would like to thank my ministry instructors, clinical supervisors, former directors and fellow chaplains for introducing me to this enriching aspect of pastoral ministry and for shaping my practice of it: Dr. Jim Beyer (1940-2007); Dr. Joe Brumfield; Rev. Terry Holley (1952-2014); Rev. Dr. David C. Johnson, BCC; Rev. Vern McNear, BCC; Dr. Ken Neller (1954-2013); Rev. Doug Pendleton; and Rev. Dr. Rick Wilson, BCC. It is my hope that what follows is a testament to their legacy of care and faithfulness to Christ and the church.

Finally, I would like to thank two of my colleagues at Kentucky Christian University. First, to Dennis Durst for asking me to craft my initial lecture on the role of chaplains in medical ethics for his bioethics course, a lecture that eventually became the article that is included in chapter 14. Then, to David Fiensy, my former dean, for asking me to construct an online course on pastoral care for our undergraduate students that has now grown into a emphasis in pastoral care within our general ministry degree program.

CHAPTER 1

# PASTORAL CARE: WHY AND WHO?

## THEOLOGY IN MINISTRY

How do you understand your place in ministry? How do you understand your place within the Church? How do you understand your place within God's salvific plan? These are the questions which are at the heart of the matter. The Church is in a state of transition in how it perceives itself and how it is perceived by the outside world. As one who has accepted the call to represent the Church, knowing *your* answers to these questions will guide you in developing your own theology (or philosophy, if it makes you more comfortable) for ministry.

To begin, there are three levels of theology that influence our place in ministry and in the Christian faith. First, there is *Practical Theology*, the reflective practitioner. For most of the history of the Church, the office of the minister was the study of God's Word. Sure, visiting the beleaguered, bereaved and backslidden was part of the daily pastoral duty, yet nothing was more important than study and reflection. However, as the numbers of the unconverted have risen over the last few centuries, a tension between activity and thought has emerged. Ministry has moved from a "being" function to a "doing" function. The pressure is to produce; there is no longer time to think about our faith or how we live out our faith. Ministry is very much "What have you done for me lately?" Thus, we are steered toward the newest fad in order to keep up with the ecclesiastical Jones.

Second, there is *Biblical Theology*. This is more than "proof-texting" or "pearl-stringing"; it is looking at the passages that influence and solidify us. It is not enough to simply know where the text is; we must know the meaning behind and around the text in order to apply it effectively to the life of faith. Here are some of the passages that have most profoundly influenced my understanding of ministry:

1

- Psalm 84:5-7—We bring water to the dying valley.
- Matthew 25:14-30—Our ministry is to the poor and marginalized.
- Mark 4:10-12—The mystery of the Gospel will be revealed to those who seek it.
- Luke 5:36-39—The old ways of doing things must be replaced with new ways.
- 2 Corinthians 5:18-21—We have been given the "ministry of reconciliation."

What are some passages that have influenced you and your decision to accept the call to ministry? We must also remember that, as we journey through life, the Bible will speak to us differently at different points in our journey. As one of my ministry professors in seminary said, "The Bible is a big book, and none of us are shaped the same way by all of it." What encourages you today may convict you tomorrow. Yet it is still God's Book, the Word of Life that guides us on our path.

Third, there is *Ecclesiastical Theology*, the theology of the congregation. Wherever we find ourselves, we must hold the balance between the ideal and the real. Many of us enter ministry with an ideal of what the Church should look like. And while we need this, we must also be realistic. We are going to suffer at the hands of people who truly believe they are doing "God's work" by executing His prophets and denying those most in need of grace. Yet, we need to aspire to the ideal lest we become programmatic and pragmatic. Learning to deal with the gap is what will make us great leaders or drive us out of ministry. We are a pilgrim Church, struggling to grasp the ideal in the real world. Most people are not spending their day trying to figure out how to live more like Jesus; they are in Church purely for selfish reasons. Thus, we must once again take up the role of Reflective Practitioner and be the presence of God to a dark and dying world.

Why is all of this important? There are three reasons. First, we live in an ever-changing culture where only the Bible is normative. There are many times when we get our cultural ideas mixed up with the Bible, replacing theology with tradition. Second, we cannot lose our true calling to institutional activity. Our calling to ministry is uniquely tailored to our personality. We cannot be someone we are not. We can only be faithful to who were are, not who a congregation wants us to be. Third, we serve a God that humbles us. Arrogance leads to destruction; however we do need a certain amount of confidence in order to be effective in ministry. If we become arrogant, it means that we are no longer teachable. As my father would say about his time in the Air Force, "You saluted everyone because you never knew who was higher up than you." Even when we serve as leaders, we must remember that we follow God.

## WHY DO WE OFFER PASTORAL CARE?

The central premise of this book revolves around two basic questions. First, what is "pastoral care?" It would seem like a simple enough question to answer, however it is one that even confuses the academic community that writes about it. Just for the fun of it, we will seek to answer this question in our next chapter. Second, how do we offer pastoral care? Naturally, we cannot answer this question without first understand what it is that we are offering. For the most part, answering this second question—both generally and specifically—will occupy the majority of our time together. It is my hope that we will engage in a pure academic exercise—you will not only be introduced to the theoretical concepts of this form of ministry, you will also gain experience through the shared experience of others. In doing so, we will seek to answer both of our questions.

Yet, there is an even more central question that is often overlooked by many writers. That question is stated in the section heading above—*Why do we offer pastoral care?* Why indeed? As many philosophers have stated, answering the question of "why" is the most central question we can answer. Thus, before we can engage any further in our study, we *must* answer the question of why we offer pastoral care. During my clinical training, my supervisor introduced three reasons for why we offer pastoral care. First, *we seek to develop community*. In his book *The Different Drum*, psychologist Scott Peck offers a deep-seeded spiritual truth that has been lost on the hustle-and-bustle, program-driven, modern Church:

> Often the most loving thing we can do when a friend is in pain is to *share* the pain—to be there even when we have nothing to offer except our presence and even when being there is painful to ourselves.[1]

---

[1] M. Scott Peck, *The Different Drum: Community Making and Peace* (New York: Touchstone Books/Simon and Schuster, 1987), 97.

Do you remember Eliphaz, Bildad, and Zophar? Of course you do, right? Well, we may not remember their names, yet we will certainly remember this story:

> Now when Job's three friends heard of all this adversity that had come upon him, they came each one from his own place, Eliphaz the Temanite, Bildad the Shuhite and Zophar the Naamathite; and they made an appointment together to come to sympathize with him and comfort him. When they lifted up their eyes at a distance and did not recognize him, they raised their voices and wept. And each of them tore his robe and they threw dust over their heads toward the sky. Then they sat down on the ground with him for seven days and seven nights with no one speaking a word to him, for they saw that his pain was very great (Job 2:11-13).[2]

Ah, now we remember them! If you are like me, you probably grew up hearing lessons in which these men were chastised for their treatment of Job, accusing him of sinning greatly against God and pleading with him to confess his sins so that his torture would end. Yet, why did they really come? The text only tells us that they came because they "heard of all this adversity that had come upon" Job. Their love for their friend was so great that they decided to visit Job. When they saw how great his suffering was, they chose to do the best thing—say nothing and share in his pain.[3] As ministers, it is our occupation to join with those who are suffering in pain, to gather around them as a community of faith and fellowship.

Second, *we seek to meet a need*. In what is probably the single best definition of what pastoral care is, Carroll Wise writes, "Pastoral care is the art of communicating the inner meaning of the gospel to persons at the point of their need."[4] This is an incredibly deep thought. First

---

[2] All references, unless otherwise noted, are from the *The New American Standard Bible*, copyright 1995 by the Lockman Foundation.

[3] It should be noted that it is not until chapter 4 than any of the friends speak, and it is only in response to Job's sorrowful soliloquy in chapter 3.

[4] Carroll A. Wise and John E. Hinkle. *The Meaning of Pastoral Care*, rev. ed. (Bloomington, IN: Meyer-Stone Books, 1989), 8.

of all, Wise describes ministry as an "art," meaning that we seek to integrate our personhood (our "being") with our ministry (our "doing"). Next, Wise reminds us that our job as ministers is not to hammer the finer points of doctrine, but to communicate the simple meaning of the Christian religion to people—that God loves them and that healing is possible through salvation. Lastly, Wise emphasizes that it is *their* need that should concern us. The situation too often goes like this: It's Thursday afternoon and there is a knock at the office door. An individual who looks quite poor has come asking for money for groceries, gas, an electric bill, etc. The minister, wanting to be evangelistic and shrewd at the same time says, "I'm sorry, there's no one here who can help you today. However, if you come back on Sunday, we can help you then." Now, I will admit that Jesus cautions us to "be shrewd as serpents and innocent as doves" in Matthew 10:16, yet the context of that passage is not about benevolence. We should never forget that the first crisis the early Church faced was in regards to benevolence—to meeting needs (Acts 6:1-6)! We are in the need-meeting business.

Third, *we seek to represent God.* It is funny how ideas flow in and out of one another. For how can we represent God if we do not seek to meet needs? One of my favorite passages—indeed, one that I ground my construct of ministry upon—is this admonition from Paul the Apostle:

> Therefore if anyone is in Christ, he is a new creature; the old things passed away; behold, new things have come. Now all these things are from God, who reconciled us to Himself through Christ and gave us the ministry of reconciliation, namely, that God was in Christ reconciling the world to Himself, not counting their trespasses against them, and He has committed to us the word of reconciliation. Therefore, we are ambassadors for Christ, as though God were making an appeal through us; we beg you on behalf of Christ, be reconciled to God. He made Him who knew no sin to be sin on our behalf, so that we might become the righteousness of God in Him (2 Corinthians 5:17-21).

*We are ambassadors for Christ!* If this is not a humbling thought, I do not know what is. We carry God's message according to the instructions that God has given us—to be honest, just, and dedicated in our service. And in order to represent God effectively, we should do the following:

- We must discern the guidance of the Holy Spirit instead of focusing on our religious sensitivities.
- We must empty ourselves of our values, attitudes, and assumptions so we can focus on the person before us who is in need.
- We must embrace whatever feelings are laid before us.
- We must not use cliché tools.
- We must remain present with people when they are in crisis.

Perhaps William Willimon said it best:

> Before the altar of God, at the bedside of the sick, in conversation with troubled souls, befuddled before the biblical text, there is the pastor. Standing in that fateful intersection between God's people and God, at that risky transaction between Christ and his Body, the church, stands the priest. It is no small thing to be in mediation between God and humanity, to offer the gifts of God's people, to intercede for the suffering of the world in prayer, rightly to divide the Word of God. With trembling and with joy, the pastor works that fateful space between here and the throne of God. . . .It is a joy to be expended in some vocation that is greater than one's self.[5]

Now that we have addressed the issue of *why* we offer pastoral care, let us turn our attention to *who* offers pastoral care.

## WHO OFFERS PASTORAL CARE?

Who has the right and privilege to minister to the hurting and distressed? Who has the right to proclaim the message of "God is love" (1 John 4:8)?

---

[5] William H. Willimon, *Pastor: The Theology and Practice of Ordained Ministry* (Nashville: Abingdon, 2002), 11.

For starters, a cursory study of the New Testament reveals that all those who receive baptism also receive a call to ministry. In the passage from 2 Corinthians 5 that we alluded above, Paul does not see a difference between clergy and laity when it comes to representing God to a dark and fallen world. Each of us who claims to be a Christian is an ambassador for Christ! As Willimon writes, "Ministry is a gift of baptism. This gift of water and the Word, this act of a descending Holy Spirit, is also an assignment. First, the baptismal gifts. Then the baptismal vocation."[6]

However, where is the place for calling to ministry in "the priesthood of all believers" (cf., Exodus 19:5-6; 1 Peter 2:5)?[7] I remember being only five or six years old when I received my call to ministry. I was visiting my grandparents in Ohio when, during the Sunday morning worship service, I remember being so inspired by the preacher's sermon that I felt that I had been called to do the same. From that moment on, I knew that my destiny was to become a minister. Over the years, I have encountered many professionals and students who have shared similar stories. Rarely have I met someone who has sustained himself or herself in ministry who has felt driven into ministry. What it comes down to is whether or not we have wrestled with what it means to pledge our lives not only to living under the shadow of the Cross but also to enlarging that shadow. Thomas Oden says that if we are able to answer such questions as can we be empathetic to the suffering of others, can we sacrifice our own desires in order to serve others, can we teach with compassion and integrity, and can we place ourselves under the scrutiny of imperfect observers, then we have most likely been called to ministry.[8] These questions are important because they remind us of something that one clinical supervisor often reminded me—ministry is not about having the right tools but about living in the presence of God. Ministry is not for the faint-hearted, especially ministry in times of crisis.

Nor is ministry confined strictly to the sanctuary. In a time that is as mobile as ours, we are seeing a shift from the dominance of the stationed minister to the dominance of the marketplace minister. Vocationally-based Christians are once again seeing themselves as ministers, seeing

---

[6] Ibid., 28.

[7] It should be noted that the phrase "the priesthood of believers" was used frequently by Martin Luther in his efforts to reform the Catholic Church.

[8] Thomas C. Oden, *Pastoral Theology: Essentials for Ministry* (New York: HarperCollins, 1982), 18-20.

their occupations as an avenue for ministry. Whether they be history professors at a state university who host a house-church, nurses who work full-time as medical missionaries, ministers who have left parish work to serve in prisons, or business men who preach for congregations part-time, Christians everywhere are making the dream of "the priesthood of all believers" a reality. It is impossible for one minister to be everywhere for everyone. Yet, with dedicated lay ministers, cups of cold water will go to those who may otherwise be overlooked.

What it comes down to is do we understand ourselves as ministers and can we operate with the authority of the Holy Spirit. The following pastoral conversation involves a minister training to be a chaplain and an elderly woman. This case study (also called a "verbatim") was presented because the minister wanted to show how much he had progressed during the training program. One of his limitations throughout the program was that he lacked not only a pastoral identity and pastoral authority but also had little understanding of himself as a person. As you read through this conversation, see if you can pick out where these concerns tripped him up.

Chaplain: May I come in?

Patient: Yes, come in.

Chaplain: Hello, I do not know if you remember me or not. I am the chaplain. I came by and talked with you before.

Patient: Yes, I remember you.

Chaplain: The last time we talked I know you were saying that you were having a difficult time. I was wondering how you were feeling today.

Patient: I am not doing good. I just want all of this to be over. I want to go home.

Chaplain: I would think it would be a terrible feeling to have pain and just wanting the pain to end.

Patient: It is just terrible. Just laying here.

Chaplain: Did you use to be very active?

Patient: Yes, I was involved in many different things.

Chaplain: That would seem difficult to be so active and now not being able to enjoy the things that you once did.

Patient: I ask myself, what is my purpose for being here?

Chaplain: I think everyone needs to feel that they have a purpose. It is not a fun place to be when you are wondering what you are here for.

Patient: You have that right.

Chaplain: I am sorry that you are going through so much right now. I do hope that your pain will end.

Patient: Thank you for your kind words. Could you please pray for me?

Chaplain: I sure will. God we come to you today. You know the pain that this woman has had to deal with. You know how she longs for this pain to end. She struggles with why she is even here on the earth. I ask God for Your comfort and peace to surround her during this time. I ask that you help to ease her burden and carry her through this. No matter what the future holds God, I ask that You make Your presence know. Pour out Your Spirit and love her through this. We ask this in Your name, All Mighty God. Amen.

Patient: Thank you. Keep me in your prayers.

Chaplain: I will. If you ever need someone just to talk to and be with you through this, there is always a chaplain here.

Patient: Thank you. You have a good day.

Chaplain: I hope your day gets better for you. Goodbye.

On the surface, this appears to be a great visit. The young chaplain carries on a decent conversation, seems to connect with her on an emotional level, and even offers a good pray that speaks to the woman's pain. Yet, therein lies the problem—he does not even know her name! As I sat through this presentation, I scribbled down lots of notes. About halfway through the presentation, I quickly jotted down in all capital letters a word that I am quite familiar with—DISCONNECTED. It is one of my biggest limitations, a hazard of being an intellectually-oriented person in a person-centered profession. After nearly nine months of training, this chaplain was still trying to impress the supervisor and our group. He was inexperienced in ministry, thus he had yet to develop any real understanding of what it meant to be a minister.

Being able to identify with the people we are serving is essential to an effective and compassionate ministry. William Arnold writes,

[T]he role of the pastor is to identify with the very people to whom we minister. In that sense, the pastor does not distance himself or herself from people according to the dictates of some other helping professions. Distance is not necessarily a bad thing as a helping act, and there may be times when the pastor must or should use it. But it is only in the context of presence that exercises of absence or distance take on special meaning. . . .We too are sinners. That provides us all with a sense of commonality and mutuality. And it is in that context that trust can develop.[9]

In addition to finding our pastoral identity and authority within our ability to identify with those to whom we minister, there are four additional concepts which will help us realize our identity and authority as ministers:

1. We must accept that ministry is not just a job; we have been called to a life *and* a lifestyle of ministry.
2. We must accept that ministry is intricately tied to a religious system. Our understanding of ministry comes out of our religious heritage and the traditions associated with that heritage.
3. We must accept that ministry is both *under* authority and *through* authority. We live under the authority of God and work through the authority that our baptism and calling offer us.
4. We must accept that ministry is an expression of who we are as a person. We cannot be someone that we are not, thus our ministry can only come through our strengths and limitations and not through another's conception.

There is little else that brings me as much joy as ministering to another, whether it is through teaching a class or praying at their bedside. There is also little else that is as challenging as ministry, whether it is responding to a massive community crisis or hugging someone who has just found out their spouse is asking for divorce. Yet, Jesus did not

---

[9] William V. Arnold, *Introduction to Pastoral Care* (Philadelphia: Westminster Press, 1982), 79.

promise us a life that would be full of roses and butterscotch pudding when He said, "If anyone wishes to come after Me, he must deny himself, and take up his cross daily and follow Me. For whoever wishes to save his life will lose it, but whoever loses his life for My sake, he is the one who will save it" (Luke 9:23-24). Let us press ahead to what lies before us!

## CHAPTER 2

# PASTORAL CARE: WHAT?

## A FUNDAMENTAL DIFFERENCE

In the previous chapter, we discussed the *why* and *who* of pastoral care. Typically, most writers who are attempting to put together a general introduction to the art of pastoral care will begin with asking *what* it is. Yet, I think to do so is limiting since many will believe that they are not qualified to perform pastoral care. I believe that any caring Christian can offer some form of pastoral care to people who are hurting and in need. Thus, I have decided to work inductively, beginning with the larger picture of why we offer pastoral care and who offers it and move down to the lower level of what pastoral care actually is.

The reason for the structure of this introductory section is because of a fundamental difference that rests between practical and academic professionals. On one hand, some professionals see "pastoral care" as a function within the discipline of pastoral counseling.[10] To these writers, the practices of hospital visitation, crisis intervention, and bereavement care are simply additional elements to the minister's overall function of counseling the beleaguered, bereaved, and backslidden. On the other hand, there are other professionals who see "pastoral care" as a discipline that includes counseling as a function.[11] To these writers, the practices

---

[10] For example, see Howard Clinebell, *Basic Types of Pastoral Care and Counseling: Resources for the Ministry of Healing and Growth*, rev. ed. (Nashville: Abingdon, 1984); Thomas C. Oden, *Pastoral Theology: Essentials for Ministry* (New York: HarperCollins, 1983); John Patton, *Pastoral Care in Context: An Introduction to Pastoral Care* (Louisville: Westminster/John Knox Press, 1993).

[11] For example, see Gerald J. Callhoun, *Pastoral Companionship: Ministry with Seriously-Ill Persons and Their Families* (New York/Mahwah, NJ: Paulist Press, 1986); Daniel H. Grossoehme, *The Pastoral Care of Children* (Binghamton, NY: Haworth Press, 1999); Larry VandeCreek, ed., *The Discipline of Pastoral Care Giving: Foundations*

of hospital visitation, crisis intervention, and bereavement care are what defines their ministry. Their purpose is to minister to the beleaguered, bereaved, and backslidden, whether it is through praying with them at the bedside of a loved one, conducting a wedding ceremony in the hospital chapel, or providing brief therapy[12] through arranged office visits.

Now, I know what some of you are thinking (other than "Why are we reading this?")—what does this have to do with our discussion? Well, my perspective is a unique one in that I have performed pastoral care on both sides of the equation. I have been a minister who saw visiting the hospital and responding to crises as part of my counseling efforts. Then, for four years, I ministered primarily as a chaplain, as one whose entire profession focuses on visiting the ill, responding to various crises, and providing short-term counseling. Both approaches have strengths and limitations, thus both approaches have value. Therefore, my goal is to develop an approach for offering effective and compassionate pastoral care that is based on the strengths of *both* approaches. To begin our descent, we will seek to answer the question of what pastoral care is by understanding the critical balance between "being" and "doing."

## UNDERSTANDING THE BALANCE

When we talk about balance in pastoral care, we are talking about the balance between "being" and "doing," between the ministry of presence and the ministry of action. The fundamental, foundational rule in pastoral care is that you allow the "patient" (this could be a family member, a hospital staff member, or a church leader) to lead. It is always uncomfortable to watch two partners dance when each of them wants to lead. It is also uncomfortable to watch two leaders try to assert their authority over the other. And it is uncomfortable to watch a minister take the lead in a pastoral conversation when the other person clearly needs to be listened to more than being told how to feel or what to do.

---

for *Outcome Oriented Chaplaincy* (New York: Binghamton, NY: Haworth Press, 2001); and Lawrence D. Reimer and James T. Wagner, *The Hospital Handbook: A Practical Guide to Hospital Visitation*, rev. ed. (Harrisburg, PA: Morehouse Publishing, 1988).

[12] Brief therapy is also known as "short-term counseling" or "solution-focused therapy." It is an unfortunate evolution in the world of managed healthcare, yet it is the world that counseling professionals now find themselves in.

The problem is that, without some self-discovery into our reasons for acting, we will instinctively drift to one of the two extremes. On one hand, there is the inclination to confuse "being present" with taking up space. For example, I was called to the bedside of a little baby that had just died on the Neonatal Intensive Care Unit (NICU). When I entered the small room, I saw the mother holding her little baby and crying. The grandmother was sitting on one side and the father on the other. Seeing little room to do much of anything, I took a spot in a corner near the entrance. After several minutes of the nurses doing what they needed to do, the mother finally noticed me. Confused, she asked me who I was and what I was doing in their room. Mentioning that I was the chaplain brought her little comfort because I was not doing anything. On the other hand, there is the inclination to confuse "offering ministry" with doing stuff. For example, one of my peers in my residency group was an experienced minister and was assigned to the surgical floor. One afternoon, he was called to the waiting area because a patient had died while in surgery. The family was spread all over the waiting area, making providing care a logistical nightmare. As he presented his case study, he talked walking around the room handing out tissues, getting coffee, gathering information, and making phone calls. Our supervisor asked him why he was so nervous in this situation. Confused by the question, our supervisor elaborated on an excellent point: even though he was an experienced minister, his default ministry setting was to "do stuff" for people in crisis rather than provide a solid pastoral presence. Instead of offering prayer and words of comfort, he offered good customer service. As you can see, it can be quite difficult to "walk the line" between "being" and "doing."

Now, I need to make something clear: I am not promoting "being" *over* "doing." Both actions are essential for effective and compassionate pastoral care. The issue at play here is the integration of both concepts— "being" and "doing"—into a cohesive construct called "pastoral care." Thus, we will continue our inductive approach by looking at this concept in broader theological terms. First, we can understand this idea of the integration of "being" and "doing" by examining the central theological concepts of *transcendence* and *immanence*. Grenz and Olsen write,

> At its best Christian theology has sought a balance between the twin biblical truths of the divine

> transcendence and the divine immanence. On the one hand, God relates to the world as the Transcendent One. That is, God is self-sufficient apart from the world. God is above the universe and comes to the world from beyond. As the Hebrew Scriptures so forcefully declare, God dwells in Heaven. . . .On the other hand, God also relates to the world as the Immanent One. This means that God is present in creation. The divine one is active within the universe, involved with the process of the world and of human history. . . .A balanced affirmation of both truths facilitates a proper relation between theology and reason or culture.[13]

Our God is a mysterious deity. In most mythical religions, the gods lived far above their worshippers, deciding it better to remain unspoiled by the filth of humanity. Yet, our God does not only live in Heaven (Ecclesiastes 5:2; Isaiah 6:1), He "is not far from each one of us" (Acts 17:27; cf., Psalm 104:29-30). The art of pastoral care can be viewed in much the same way: As Christians who have accepted our call (whether that be professional or lay ministry) through our baptism, we do live "above" those who have not. We do not do so through arrogance but through the confidence of knowing that we are living for God. Yet, we must be among those who are hurting and suffering in order to continue the ministry of the Incarnation (John 17:15-18). It is easy to lock ourselves away in our studies and never come out except to preach, yet it is also easy to be so ingrained with the people that we lose our pastoral identity.

As we continue to spiral down this construct, we come to the concepts of spirituality and religion. For most of us, there is little difference between the two. To view these two concepts in this way is to engage in theological naivety. Thus, how do we differentiate between the two? First, spirituality is that sense of that God "has planted eternity in the human heart" (Ecclesiastes 3:11, NLT). I am convinced that God created us to yearn to *be* in relationship with Him. Thus, from a pastoral care perspective, the *being* nature of spirituality—of being in relationship with God—informs our understanding of presence in ministry. Second,

---

[13] Stanley J. Grenz and Roger E. Olsen, *20th-Century Theology: God and the World in a Transitional Age* (Downers Grove, IL: InterVarsity Press, 1992), 11-12.

religion becomes not how we *define* our spirituality but how we *practice* our spirituality. Winfried Corduan defines religion as "a system of beliefs and practices that provide values to give life meaning and coherence by directing a person towards transcendence."[14] As one of my psychiatric patients once said, "Religion is the cup that holds our spirituality." We cannot have one without the other. Spirituality is about how we perceive truth and how we find that truth in paradoxes. We need religion because it provides us with the necessary structure to investigate our spirituality. Thus, from a pastoral care perspective, the *doing* nature of religion—of engaging in sacred rituals and partaking of sacred sacraments—informs our understanding of action in ministry.

To conclude our spiral, we come to the concepts of presence and action, the work of the minister himself or herself. Although we are still talking about the "being" and "doing" of the minister, I find that John Patton's designations are quite illuminating. Although he is one of the writers who approaches this subject from a pure counseling perspective, Patton has much to offer us. Specifically, Patton offers us the ideas of the "ministry of availability" and "ministry of introduction."[15] For Patton, the minister is to always be available, always ready to respond regardless of his or her condition. This fits well with our understanding of "being." During my residency, I had a terrible weekend, one in which I literally had no time to sleep because there was so much going on in the hospital. In my final eight hours of the full-weekend shift, I was paged to five traumas and three deaths. It did not matter that I had not slept in three days. It did not matter that I was physically exhausted. I was the minister on-call, thus I had to be ready to respond to whatever came my way. True ministry cannot be planned, thus we must always be prepared to provide ministry. Also, the minister serves as a resource—the "ministry of introduction." In Patton's original concept, the "ministry of introduction" seeks to introduce troubled persons to resources (agencies, programs, etc.) that can help the counselee in some way.[16] In my concept, I see the "ministry of introduction" in a little different light. I see this as more of a teaching function rather than a social action function,

---

[14] Winfried Corduan, *Neighboring Faiths: A Christian Introduction to World Religions* (Downers Grove, IL: InterVarsity Press, 1998), 21.

[15] Patton, *Pastoral Care in Context*, 220-226.

[16] Wayne E. Oates is actually the one who defined this aspect of the minister's mission; see *The Christian Pastor* (Philadelphia: Westminster, 1964), 220-221.

although I do not deny its value. In pastoral care situations, the minister does not act as a social worker but as a shepherd. And as a shepherd, we are to guide the wandering sheep. Thus, our "ministry of introduction" may be more alike the line of teaching burdened souls how to engage in the disciplines of prayer, confession and forgiveness, and how to benefit from the sacraments of baptism and communion. Once we realize that pastoral care—in truth, ministry in general—is not about one or the other but about the integration of both, then we will be able to adequately walk the line between "being" and "doing."

## THE BALANCING ACT

Knowing when to "be present" and when to "do something" is a tricky business. In my experience in dealing with families in crisis, I have yet to discover a system for gauging how a family is coping in a given trauma. Some do not want a minister present, some do not want the minister to leave, some are thankful for the routine updates without the minister hanging around, and some see the minister as keeping them from their loved one. Remember my example from above about the time I stood in a corner and watched a mother helplessly cry over her child? It is hard to deny that I was present for that particular crisis. After all, I take up a decent amount of room. Yet, I was not really present with that mother in her time of need. I did not offer the gospel to that woman. I was physically present; however I was pastorally absent. Kenneth Mottram says that "being present" does not mean that we cling to people like shadows. He says that "being present" means that we will "stay with them throughout the time they are in crisis."[17] What this commitment does is give us the freedom to do our job, to minister to the patient and/ or family in whatever way they need.

What exactly does this commitment entail? To answer this question, we turn to William Arnold, and his discussion on the functions of a minister.[18] First, the minister comes as a *representative*. When we do, we represent God (to all), the community of faith (to the patient/family), and the patient/family (to the medical staff). Second, the minister

---

[17] Kenneth P. Mottram, *Caring for Those in Crisis: Facing Ethical Dilemmas with Patients and Families* (Grand Rapids, MI: Brazos Press, 2007), 145.
[18] William V. Arnold, *Introduction to Pastoral Care* (Philadelphia: Westminster, 1982), 86-98.

comes as a *servant*. When we come as a servant, we offer our skills to the service of the one who needs us. We serve by praying, listening to those in crisis, offering forgiveness and repentance, administering sacraments, and advocating for the patient. Third, the minister comes as a *carrier of tradition*. When we do, we bring with us the traditional roles of healer (James 5:14), sustainer (Psalm 84:5-7), counselor (2 Timothy 2), and reconciler (2 Corinthians 5:17-21). By engaging in these roles when needed, we humbly yet confidently assert our pastoral authority and pastoral identity. In doing so, we remind the patient and/or family member that we are present *and* they are being cared for. If we keep these thoughts in mind when we seek to minister to those in our care, we will do a good job. We may not win any "Minister of the Year" awards, but our people will know that they are cared for. In our next chapter, we will conclude our introductory section by asking ourselves the questions of how, when and where do we offer pastoral care.

CHAPTER 3

# PASTORAL CARE: WHEN AND WHERE?

## THE "WHEN?" OF PASTORAL CARE

Overall, this is an easy one. When we are asked to go, we go! Period. If someone asks us to see them or if someone asks us to see someone else, we should respect the urgency of the request, especially when it is regarding a crisis situation. If you remember from the last chapter, one of John Patton's elements of quality pastoral care is the "ministry of availability."[19] By this, he means that the minister or pastoral care giver should be flexible with his or her schedule, as a call to a member's home or to the hospital can come at a moment's notice and could require a great deal of attention. One of the beauties of being a chaplain was that my schedule was dictated to me by fours things: my pager, my phone, my printer, and my own initiative. As long as none of the first three go off, then I was at my leisure to visit whomever I wanted. Yet, when the call came in, I *had* to respond, and usually within fifteen minutes.

In the congregational setting, there is the sense that a minister should drop whatever he or she is doing and respond to the call. Care must be taken here because we may be shirking other duties if we become "drop of a hat" types. With the exception of a death, most calls can wait until we have finished our responsibilities, should we be working our way through a counseling session, a visitation round, or preparing a lesson. Even in my hospital work, I often had to prioritize my crises. There were several times when I had to decide which was more important between a death on the ICU where no family is expected to arrive, a death on one of

---

[19] John Patton, *Pastoral Care in Context: An Introduction to Pastoral Care* (Louisville: Westminster/John Knox Press, 1993), 220.

the non-critical units where family is present, a trauma in the Emergency Room, and a patient on our long-term rehab unit that had requested prayer. Each of these situations required my attention because each of them required that a consult be completed. Thus, I had to take the time to prioritize my visits—taking into account that chaos knows neither schedules nor intentions. The same principle can apply to congregational work as well.

So how would I answer the question of when I should visit someone? First, we must answer the question of whether this is a "crisis" visit or a "routine" visit. By "crisis," I mean a situation when a death has occurred, when someone has been involved in an accident and is being taken to a local hospital for treatment, when someone has attempted suicide, when there has been domestic violence, or when a patient's health has taken a turn for the worst. There are other situations, of course; however these are the primary situations. By "routine," I mean a situation where continued pastoral care is offered (e.g., a nursing home visit or someone who is ill at home), or where a new relationship may be formed (i.e., we are asked by one of our members to visit someone from outside the congregation). When I was once serving as a youth minister for a congregation in Texas, the staff ministers were required each week to visit three ladies at two different nursing homes. One of the ladies was in a complete vegetative state and another had succumbed to complete dementia. The third, however, was still quite sharp, and probably provided me with as much pastoral care as I provided to her. As a young minister in a troubled congregation, her visits were often the highlight of my week. To call them "routine" visits is, certainly, misleading because it is often in the "routine" visits that God reveals Himself more clearly. Thus we should never treat a "routine" visit as "routine."

Once we have established the priority of the situation, we develop our agenda for visiting the person and/or family. As I said above, in the hospital setting, I had fifteen minutes to respond to each crisis. If I was in a situation that prevented me from responding in that amount of time, it was my responsibility to contact the unit and inform them of my delay. In congregational work, I would suggest that, when a crisis situation arises, you make an effort to arrive within one hour of the call. This allows time for the situation to fully develop. It also gives us time to take care of business. We may have to cancel appointments, reschedule meetings, or put off some study. *This is okay!* When I first entered into ministry many years ago, it was difficult to take off at a moment's notice and attend to an emergency. However, thanks to all of the recent advancements in technology, we are only a text message away from clearing our schedules.

Yet, what if the situation is not really an emergency? Yes, Mrs. Jones is in the hospital, and yes she will have surgery, but do we really need to go this moment? Unless the situation fits into one of the ones listed above, the visit can really wait. I would suggest that "routine" visits, when requested, be made within twenty-four hours of the request. You will also want to take into consideration your situation before embarking on such a visit. Is this a visit you could add to a regularly scheduled day of visiting? Do you need to make special considerations due to the distance that you will have to travel? One question you can never ask is if someone else would be more qualified or more appropriate to make the visit. *If we have been personally requested, then it falls to us and us alone to make the visit!* I have been both an associate minister and a senior/preaching minister. There have been times when I was requested instead of the senior minister to make a visit, and there have been times when the associate minister was asked instead of me to visit someone. We are asked because the person asking—whether they are asking for themselves or for someone else—respects us enough to trust us with this situation. There are only two instances when it is ever appropriate to refer to someone else: 1) when the nature of the visit falls outside our scope of practice (i.e., visiting a patient in a psychiatric facility when we have no such background), or 2) when we are honestly unavailable (i.e., we are on vacation and someone in the congregation dies). In all other circumstances, it is our responsibility to go when we are called.

Before we leave this section, I would like to briefly discuss some practical matters regarding requested visits. There have been a number of times when members have come to me and asked me to visit a friend or family member who is in the hospital, nursing home, or rehab facility. I have found that these requests almost always have an underlying reason—our church member is not confident in the salvation of their friend or family member, so they ask us to go an evangelize that person. As we will see, we have many goals in offering pastoral care to others. *Proselytizing is never one of them*! If the person wants to talk about their salvation, then that is acceptable. However, we can never force our religious beliefs on another or come to them in the name of the Lord in such an underhanded or arrogant way. Yet, we still go because we have been asked to. Now, it is important to remember that this person is not under our direct pastoral influence. She or he may have their own minister and their own community of faith. Thus, we are to respect this. It is also possible that the person we have been requested to see does not want pastoral care. We are to also respect this. As one of my former chaplain colleagues once told me, we go and let the person we are visiting guide our activity. Regardless of the outcome, we are to report back to our member, remembering privacy concerns, the nature of our visit. If the person has his or her own minister or refuses our care, we are under no obligation to visit again. Yet, if an opportunity is present, then we should continue visiting this person for as long as is necessary.

## THE "WHERE?" OF PASTORAL CARE

There is a lot that I hope you get from this book. Primarily, I hope that you will develop an understanding for what pastoral care is and how to provide it in certain specific situations. Yet, there is something else that I hope you get from this—that, as Christians, the whole of our life is about ministry. It has been a popular topic over the last twenty to thirty years to talk about vocation, about members seeing themselves as ministers in their chosen professions (i.e., seeing oneself as a Christian teacher instead of a teacher who is also a Christian). The hope is that this will engender a sense of mission within all Christians, that we will become domestic missionaries in a Church that is saturated with foreign missionaries. Some faith-based colleges and universities have even developed academic programs (typically referred to as "vocational ministry" or "tentmaker" programs) for students who are interested in planting new congregations or ministering to congregations while supporting themselves primarily through some type of professional careers. The goal of such programs is to help Christians see all of life as ministry, to understand that anyone who "gives even a cup of cold water" (Matthew 10:42) is participating in the reconciling work of Christ (2 Corinthians 5:17-21). Paul Stevens writes,

> There is no need to be "called" through an existential compelling experience to an occupation in society. God gives motivation and gift. God guides. Work, family, civil vocation and neighbouring are encompassed in our

total response to God's saving and transforming call in Jesus. . . .So vocational guidance is not discerning our "call" but, in the context of our call to discipleship, holiness and service (now to be considered), discerning the guidance of God in our lives and learning how to live in every dimension to please him.[20]

What I hope you glean from this is that *every encounter is an opportunity for us to provide pastoral care to someone.* Do you want to know the true secret to church growth? This is the one that everyone knows but no one wants to accept. The secret to church growth is friendship. Now the secret to church development is a whole different story, yet the simplest way to grow a congregation is to learn the art of friend-making. I think David Hansen is correct in saying that

Many pastoral responsibilities fall under the rubric *friend.* Hospital calls, home visits and time spent with parishioners are all acts of friendship. . . .Good chaplains know how to become a friend. Nobody needs a religious professional. Normal people don't even like them. But everyone wants a friend—a friend is a gift from God. A friend is a parable of Jesus. . . .Whether the mission of the visit is to bring encouragement, to admonish, or to share joy or tragedy, it is the visit of a friend and is thereby enacted grace.[21]

Simply listening to a friend who is having a bad day and then praying for them is a form of pastoral care. As Dietrich Bonhoeffer writes, "A Christian fellowship lives and exists by the intercession of its members; one for another, or it collapses."[22] Some of the best pastoral care that I ever provided has come through random conversations after a service or

[20] R. Paul Stevens, *The Other Six Days: Vocation, Work, and Ministry in Biblical Perspective* (Grand Rapids, MI/Cambridge, England/Vancouver, BC: Eerdmans/Regent College Publishing, 1999), 82-83.

[21] David Hansen, *The Art of Pastoring: Ministry Without All the Answers* (Downers Grove, IL: InterVarsity Press, 1994), 121-122.

[22] Dietrich Bonhoeffer, *Life Together,* trans. John W. Doberstein (New York: Harper and Row, 1954), 86.

at the mall. When it comes to caring for one another, we are never off the clock. This is how I understand the connection of vocation and ministry: It is the Church's vocation to minister to people through caring for people. As theologian Gilbert Bilezikian writes, "At no time does the church resemble more the Savior than when it emulates him in self-giving servanthood in response to situations of human need."[23] Pastoral care cannot involve "one-time encounters" where we pray with someone and then leave them to their own devices; our caring for one another must be a continual activity.

So how do we answer the question of "where" do we offer pastoral care? The answer is anywhere and everywhere, just like the answer to our previous question is any time and every time. Whether it is a call to the hospital, to a nursing home, in the foyer of the church building, or while walking from the library to the cafeteria, any time we are offered an opportunity to share the love of Christ with someone, we should answer the call to do so. In our next chapter, we will look at how to provide pastoral care in the traditional context of a hospital or nursing home. We will also examine some considerations for making home visits. This will prepare us for transitioning into the remainder of our emphasis on ministering in times of crisis.

---

[23] Gilbert Bilezikian, *Christianity 101: Your Guide to Eight Christian Beliefs* (Grand Rapids, MI: Zondervan, 1993), 217.

# CHAPTER 4

# PASTORAL CARE: HOW?

In this final chapter, we will seek to answer the "how" question about pastoral care. I should clarify something however: this chapter will not consist of a "how-to"/technique discussion, but a discussion regarding the process and flow of a pastoral encounter.

When I decided to participate in my clinical training, I did so because I thought Clinical Pastoral Education (CPE) would teach me *how to be a chaplain.* I was operating out of a "checklist mentality" approach to ministry. For example, I believed CPE would teach me what to do exactly when ministering to a family at a death or what to pray for when called to a patient's bedside. This, I believe, was my programmed response to ministry education because it was how I was trained in college. In my ministry training, I was given an outline of how to visit a patient who was in the hospital or nursing home. As I would visit someone, I would work through this "mental checklist," making sure that I had completed my task of visitation (e.g., ask them how they are doing, respond empathetically, pray, and shake their hand on the way out). It was not until I found myself in my first real crisis as a chaplain—three pediatric deaths in twenty-fours hours two weeks into my program— that I realized the value of presence over action and that *I* was not in control of the encounter.

However, pastoral care is about building, developing, and strengthening relationships. As many of my students and fellow colleagues have mentioned, most of their experiences with pastoral care have not been in crisis situations, but have been in "routine" encounters with people that they worship with. This should help us understand that "pastoral care" happens whenever one concerned Christian engages another Christian about what is going on in his or her life. As Gary Collins writes,

> The body of Christ has tremendous potential for providing the kind of fellowship, acceptance, feeling of belonging, and security that brings great therapeutic value, both to believers and to other needy people who come into contact with believers. The New Testament uses the Greek word *koinonia* to describe this kind of fellowship. It involves Christians sharing together, bearing one another's burdens, confessing faults to each other, mutually submitting, encouraging one another, and building each other up as we walk with the Lord. In one word, Christian fellowship is the continual expression of *love*.[24]

As we discussed earlier, the rite of baptism "ordains" every Christian to the ministry of pastoral care, although some Christians are more gifted to provide pastoral care than others. Yet, as Collins stated above, our love for one another compels us to minister to one another. Remember the words of Jesus?

> This is My commandment, that you love one another, just as I have loved you. Greater love has no one than this, that one lay down his life for his friends. You are My friends if you do what I command you. No longer do I call you slaves, for the slave does not know what his master is doing; but I have called you friends, for all things that I have heard from My Father I have made known to you. You did not choose Me but I chose you, and appointed you that you would go and bear fruit, and *that* your fruit would remain, so that whatever you ask of the Father in My name He may give to you. This I command you, that you love one another (John 15:12-17).

Thus, we will focus on the relationship that evolves during a pastoral encounter. It is important that we engrain this because we will never truly care for someone if we are always fretting about what to "do" next. In order

---

[24] Gary R. Collins, *How to Be a People Helper*, rev. ed. (Wheaton, IL: Tyndale, 1995), 170.

to conceptualize pastoral care as a process, I will introduce you to what my former supervisor called the "communication spiral" that governs pastoral encounters. Next, we will look at a very special group that requires our attention—children. Then, we will conclude with a discussion of the tools that are available to the minister or pastoral care provider.

## THE COMMUNICATION SPIRAL[25]

First and foremost, when we enter into a pastoral encounter, we must remember that we are entering into a situation that is unique, challenging, and spiritual. Most traditional ministry training focuses on doing something. "After all, it's only through doing something that ministers know they are worth anything," some will say. Yet, when we engage someone who is confined to a hospital bed or to a family who is in the midst of a crisis, sacred-sounding sentiments and liturgical libations are meaningless. This is why Katie Maxwell writes, "To be confident in the visiting ministry you must begin with prayer, feed on information, and then act on faith."[26] To do any less would be to violate the sanctity of the pastoral relationship. Above all else, we must remember that pastoral care takes place within the context of a relationship. As I have said already, it may be a relationship that is beginning or one that is ongoing. Yet—and here's the important part—it is a *pastoral* relationship. And, as with any other type of relationship, it follows a process:

### PASTORAL CHITCHAT

This is the beginning stage of the relational conversation. Conversations in this stage usually last less than fifteen minutes, and it is at this stage that introductions or re-introductions are made. Not much happens in this stage, and, to be honest, most pastoral encounters will fall within this stage. Here is an example of many of the conversations that I have had with people in the Emergency Room:

---

[25] This paradigm was developed by Rev. David C. Johnson, DMin, BCC, my CPE supervisor.

[26] Katie Maxwell, *Bedside Manners: A Practical Guide to Visiting the Ill* (Grand Rapids, MI: Baker, 1990), 13.

Chaplain: Hello, my name is Rob and I'm one of the chaplains. I was coming around to see how you are feeling tonight.

Patient: Oh, thank you. I'm not feeling real well tonight. I guess if I was, I wouldn't be here. Right?

Chaplain: Yes, that's true.(It is usually at this stage that some form of simple conversation begins about the game that is on television, whether or not we know another minister, or how well they have been cared for.)

Chaplain: Is there anything I can do for you tonight?

Patient: (1) No, there's not really anything else. Thank you for coming.
(2) Sure, you could pray for me, if you'd like.
(3) No, but could you (check with the nurse about something).

Chaplain: (1) Well, I hope you get to feeling better. May God bless you.
(2) Sure, I would love to pray for you. (Offer prayer.)
(3) Not a problem. I hope you get to feeling better.

So what distinguishes this conversation as "pastoral?" Heije Faber and Ebel van der Schoot write, "In all pastoral conversation, the primary aim of the pastor is to help the other person see his life in God's light."[27] Does this mean that as long as we pray or introduce ourselves as a minister, then the conversation is "pastoral?" Does it mean that I am not as crazy as I sound when I say that anyone who goes to another on behalf of God and the Church is offering "pastoral care?" Well, yes and yes. Aside from the offer to pray (if it is requested or accepted), what distinguishes this conversation as "pastoral" is the introduction of the visitor as a minister, as a representative of God. We may not engage into deep theological conversations about theodicy; however we will have shared God's love with those in need.

## PASTORAL CONVERSATION

In this stage of the conversation, we actually move into a legitimate conversation. Whereas in chitchat we talk about mostly superficial topics, we move into proclamation when we enter into this stage of the conversation. As Dietrich Bonhoeffer writes,

---

[27] Heije Faber and Ebel van der Schoot, *The Art of Pastoral Conversation: Effective Counseling through Personal Encounter* (Nashville: Abingdon, 1965), 115.

> The mission of spiritual care falls under the general mission of proclamation. Caring for the soul is a special sort of proclamation. The minister should proclaim whenever possible. The minister is the pastor, that is, the shepherd of the congregation which needs daily care (2 Tim. 4:2).[28]

Spiritual care in times of crisis and complacency helps us to hear the Word of God in times of correction and conviction. In offering the Word of God, we do not necessarily recite Scripture, although the use of Scripture reading may be used. In this thought comes the concept that proclamation is not only preaching or reading Scripture but is the "in-breaking" of God into the world. In this stage of the conversation, we serve as more than a representative of God and of the Church; *we become the continuation of the Incarnation.* It is during this stage that we must ask and answer the question "Why am I here?" If we can answer this question with an answer other than "to make a pastoral visit," then we have fully moved in pastoral conversation and are looking at moving into pastoral counseling.

## PASTORAL COUNSELING

Now, it is important to understand that I am not talking about psychotherapy here. What I mean by "pastoral counseling" is the sacred discipline of tending to soul of a hurting person. In the act of pastoral visitation, there is no room for Freudian psychology; there is no place for psychoanalysis because we are not there to analyze the person or psychologize their situation. As Bonhoeffer exhorts us, we are not to take a "calculating or investigative approach" in pastoral care.[29] This does not mean that the practice of psychology is lost on pastoral care for the fundamental principles of Carl Roger's "person-centered" approach are quite beneficial to pastoral care. Here are the three principles in brief:[30]

---

[28] Dietrich Bonhoeffer, *Spiritual Care*, trans. Jay C. Rochelle (Philadelphia: Fortress Press, 1985), 30.

[29] *Ibid*, 36.

[30] For a good introduction to Roger's theory, see Nathaniel J. Raskin, Carl R. Rogers, and Marjorie C. Witty, "Client-Centered Therapy," in *Current Psychotherapies*, 9th ed., edited by Raymond J. Corsini and Danny Wedding (Belmont, CA: Brooks/Cole, 2011),

1. *Congruence*—If we are not genuine in our purpose, then we have no purpose visiting this person. In addition, our words and actions must not only match but must also align with the teachings of Scripture and the Christian religion.

2. *Empathy*—When we are empathetic, we share in the emotions that are presented to us. We do not add to them or diminish them; we creatively participate in the emotional experience without succumbing to it or suppressing it.

3. *Unconditional Positive Regard*—Here we suspend our judgment of the other and engage them with the respect that they deserve. As Faber and van der Schoot remind us, the situation may not make sense to us, yet it is what it is and an opportunity to minister has been presented to us.[31]

It is the last concept that is vital to this stage of the pastoral conversation, and to pastoral care as a whole. What is of importance here is to remember that the person to whom we are ministering has within them the strength and resources to initiate growth and change. It is not our responsibility to "fix" the person or the situation, an incredibly difficult reality for ministers to accept. Our role, therefore, is to guide the person "to take the real responsibility for [his or her] own life and decisions."[32] We are only a guide; we are people-helpers, not people-fixers or problem-solvers. Most people can solve their own problems. Those who cannot are likely outside our scope of practice and should be referred accordingly.

There is a danger to be aware of as we engage in pastoral counseling. And it is a death-nail that practically all care-givers are guilty of using at least once in their careers—personalizing a situation. For example, I was called one morning to the surgery area where a family had just been informed that their 21-year-old son had died during surgery. The nursing supervisor was already present, as I had been with another similar situation on the Pediatric ICU. Most of the conversation is hazy

---

148-195. See also Roger's own works, primarily *Client-Centered Therapy: Its Current Practice, Implications, and Theory* (London: Constable, 1951), and *On Becoming a Person: A Therapist's View of Psychotherapy* (London: Constable, 1961).

[31] Faber and van der Schoot, *The Art of Pastoral Conversation*, 67.

[32] Ibid., 74.

because I was more present than active. However, I remember at one point the nursing supervisor attempting to connect with the family by letting them know that she had lost a child before. Unfortunately, this attempt was met with contempt. The father shot back how old her child was when she lost him, and she admitted that the child was only an infant. "Well, that's not the same as losing a 21-year-old, is it?" Now it is important to remember that, in the early stages of shock and grief, people will react in ways that are abnormal for them. They may lash out physically or verbally in ways that will surprise both us and them. However, it is also important to remember that personalizing an issue shifts the focus from them to us. When the father lashed out at the nursing supervisor he was, in effect, pleading for her to focus on him and his pain. He even later apologized for what he had said to her. I will admit that personalizing is a limitation of mine. During my clinical training, I was assigned to the pediatric units. It made sense since I was a father with two young children. For the most part, I found that personalizing helped me empathize more. Yet, I also found it to be dangerous when my attempts at personalization offended parents in their time of need. When we are in such situations where the urge to connect on a personal level arises, let us remember these words of wisdom: "Proper distance helps establish proper closeness."[33]

In this stage of the process, it is important to remember two things. First, if the person wants to talk, you cannot stop them from talking. Second, if the person does not want to talk, there is nothing we can do to get them to talk. It is important to ask ourselves how comfortable we are with silence. It is a common misconception that ministers should engage everyone they meet with in conversation. Yet there are times when words may be inappropriate, when even prayer may be inappropriate. Again Bonhoeffer admonishes us to remember that the task of the minister "is to listen and the parishioner's is to talk. The pastor's duty in this form of spiritual care may be to be silent for a long time in order to become free of all 'priestly' behavior and conceited clericalism."[34] While the

---

[33] Ibid., 37.

[34] Bonhoeffer, *Spiritual Care*, 31. For more on the arts of listening and guiding conversations, see Collins, *How to Be a People Helper*, 38-52; and Douglas Purnell, *Conversation as Ministry: Stories and Strategies for Confident Caregiving* (Cleveland, OH: Pilgrim Press, 2003).

use of exploratory questions is, at time, useful to help begin or guide a conversation, it should be remembered that our role is to *respond* to what is offered to us, not to force a conversation. As I have said already, sometimes just being there is enough. Coincidently, our presence is what leads us into the final stage of the conversation process—pastoral communion.

## PASTORAL COMMUNION

This is the most difficult of the four stages to talk about because it is neither our goal to get here nor is there any way of gauging whether the conversation will go this route. It just happens. I was visiting with an older woman on our extended therapy unit after being asked to visit her roommate. We had a pleasant conversation that included her asking me if I knew a particular minister, prayer, a conversation about ecclesiological differences and similarities between our respective traditions, and her expressing her concerns about her roommate's health. Then the conversation simply stopped. After a moment's pause, she turned to me and smiled. There was nothing left to say in that particular instance. I wished her blessings and farewell. Without meaning to, she and I had entered into true communion with God.

Our goal is not to get to this level. If we are actively listening to someone, he or she will get here on their own. As we attend to what they are saying, we create a sacred space where they can feel safe to share their spiritual concerns. As we actively empathize, they will follow our lead and seek the healing and comforting strength that our presence as God's representatives offers. As we work with them in naming their pain and accepting their condition, they will find themselves experiencing feelings and recalling memories that they had repressed or forgotten about. Thus, our job is to help them experience God and find comfort in this anxious situation, not to find out if they are okay with Jesus. Just as Moses found himself on holy ground before God (Exodus 3:1-6), we will find ourselves confronted by a holy and righteous God who compels us to honor His sovereignty and respond to Him in such a way that shows we respect His presence. When we get to Holy Ground, we will find that there are no words appropriate to say. However, once we start talking, we leave Holy Ground and return to the chitchat stage of the conversation. It is almost awkward when we realize that we have left Holy Ground. It is not because we have done anything incorrect, but because we have been in presence of God.

## A WORD ABOUT MINISTERING TO CHILDREN AND TEENAGERS

Although we will spend some time in the next section discussing the pastoral care of children, I could not allow myself to leave this section without saying at lease something about it. Most ministers approach ministering to children in one of these two ways. First, ministers will ignore the child and minister solely to the adults present. Second, ministers will be so overcome with anxiety at the thought of ministering to children that they will avoid or ignore the situation totally. When they actually do buck up the courage to minister to children, they usually do so by either "talking up" to the child (treating them like an adult regardless of their age) or "talking down" to them (treating them like a helpless infant regardless of their age). Any of these responses, of course, is disrespectful not only of our calling to ministry but also of the sanctity of children as creations of God.

Before I entered into my clinical training, the thought of visiting a child at the hospital horrified me. What would I say to the parents? How could I justify an image of God that is powerful and loving to people who are looking over their child who is hooked up to a breathing machine? Why if the child dies? These are certainly questions that we may encounter in our pastoral care-giving, and they are certainly not questions that can wait until we are in the situation in order to answer them. As Daniel Grossoehme writes, our understanding of a child's place in this world is found in the fact that one mother knew that her son was destined to die for all of mankind:

> Care for God's youngest children is rooted here in the act of thanksgiving for the gift of children. Jewish theology is rooted in the adoption of the Hebrews as God's chosen children; the Scriptures bear witness to their developing understanding of what that meant. Christians believe that God gave humanity the gift of a child in Christ. For them, this is the child that breaks open the cycles of life and time. Christians who give thanks for that Child

can ground themselves in that thanksgiving to seek and
serve Christ in the children around them today.[35]

Thus, our ministry to children and teenagers must be conducted
within the same frame of congruence, empathy, and unconditional
positive regard as with adults.

## TOOLS OF THE TRADE

Before we conclude this chapter, let me briefly discuss some of the "tools"
that are at the minister's disposal. It should be remembered that these
"tools" are only to be used in addition to our presence, our listening and
attending, and our calling. Our greatest "tools" are two we probably
would not think of in our "doing"-oriented profession—our story of
faith, and our practice of spirituality. These two "tools" alone will provide
us with more direction and more strength than any other "tool" that we
may use. Yet, we are often asked to use some of the following "tools" in
our work, in order to bring comfort to the patient, the family, or both.

- *Prayer*—Prayer is the universal tool that any minister or pastoral
  care-giver can use. However, we must be careful not to generalize,
  exaggerate, analyze, moralize, or dogmatize the problem simply
  by saying, "Let's prayer about it." We must first take the time to
  listen to the person while speaking to God on their behalf. We
  will talk more about the place of prayer in the pastoral visit later.
- *Scripture Reading*—Reading the Word of God to people in crisis
  can have a great soothing effect. It can offer them words of
  comfort in times of despair, or it can give words to their anger
  and anxiety. What is most important is to offer readings that are
  appropriate to the situation (i.e., reading Psalm 30 to someone
  who finds their faith challenged by their illness). The *Common
  Book of Prayer* is an excellent resource for relevant prayers and
  Scripture readings.
- *Communion*—Protestants practice few sacraments, and few
  sacraments connect us to Christ more than Communion. For

---

[35] Daniel H. Grossoehme, *The Pastoral Care of Children* (New York: Haworth Pastoral
Press/Haworth Press, Inc., 1999), 1.

it is through the taking of the bread and the cup that we are reminded that "by His wounds you were healed" (1 Peter 2:24; cf., Isaiah 53:5). It may seem archaic, but I recommend that you take a portable Communion kit with you for pastoral visits on Sundays.

- *Anointing*—Although it is not a sacrament practiced by most Protestants, the sacrament of anointing the sick can be comforting. In the "Parable of the Good Samaritan," the Samaritan "anointed" the wounds of the injured man, treating his injuries (Luke 10:33-34). It may not seem like much to most of us, yet, for some, having a few drops of oil dabbed on their foreheads is equivalent to being touched by the Divine. Most Pastoral Care offices will have oil available.

- *Repentance/Confession*—There will be times when people, in their illness, will seek reconciliation for the things they have done in their lives. Baptism does not always wash away the stain of sin for some. When faced with a terminal illness, people will reach down in the deep recesses of their soul and bring forth dark secrets that they have long hidden. In our presence, we serve as intermediary between the troubled soul and God. We walk with them through the path towards forgiveness, towards peace and a clear conscience.

- *Baptism*—It is not in my theology to require the practice for infants and children, yet I have found that this often brings comfort to grieving parents. We also find ourselves being asked to baptize an adult. For those who practice immersion, this can be tricky in a hospital setting. The issue of baptism is one of those issues that may require us to stretch ourselves doctrinally.

There are some other "tools" that we can use, like placing prayer cloths on the bed of the sick or making sure there are enough tissues (never underestimate this one in times of sorrow); however these are the primary ones. Again, it is important to remember that these "tools" are only to be used to strengthen our ministry, not become our ministry. It is through your story and your expression of faith that you will find your energy and direction for providing pastoral care to those in need.

## CHAPTER 5

# CRISIS THEORY

## THEOLOGY OF CRISIS

If I were to be asked what my favorite book of the Bible is, I would most likely say that it is the Gospel of Mark. I enjoy Mark's "quick-fire" narrative about Jesus' life and ministry. Yet, if I were to really search my feelings, I would probably have to say that Psalms is my favorite book. It has often been said that you can experience every emotion in Psalms. One of the reasons why I enjoy studying Psalms (and inflicted my love for Psalms on others through sermons) is because there is a real-ness to the prayers that are uttered in those pages. They are full of emotion, full of life. The poets do not hold back in both praise and pain, casting their cares before God in hymnic fashion as they extol and admonish their Creator and Sustainer.

One psalm that has been of particular value to me has been Psalm 30. Early on, it was more of an academic interest in the nature and rhetoric of the psalm, as I could not truly resonate with the deep-seated anguish that reverberates through the prayer. Yet, life has taught me a thing or two (or maybe seven or eight things), and now I feel more connected to the psalm than ever before. I believe that the message of the psalm actually begins in v. 6-7, where the poet is extolling God for providing for him:

> [6]Now as for me, I said in my prosperity, "I will never be moved." [7]O LORD, by Your favor You have made my mountain to stand strong; You hid Your face, I was dismayed.

Do you see what happened? Normally, I would refrain from using the verse notations, but I think here it is important. In v. 6-7a, the poet extols God for building him up. Yet, in the second half of v. 7, he cries out to God because he now senses that God is distant from him. Crisis has entered his life, in the time that it takes to write a semicolon.

This is exactly how crisis enters our lives. In one moment, we are living the dream; in the next moment, we are lamenting the nightmare. As we continue to walk through the poet's petition, we find that he has called out to God—repeatedly it seems, yet with no answer. Thus we find that *every* crisis is theological and spiritual in nature because in *every* crisis we come face-to-face with two stark realities: 1) our own frailty as humans; and 2) our perception of God may be off. With regard to the first reality, Ernest Becker says that in crisis (and in his context, death is the great crisis that all must endure) we realize that we have believed a lie.[36] We have believed that humans are capable of overcoming any obstacle, including death itself. Unfortunately, when the rubber meets the road (and I cannot believe that I actually used that cliché), we are crushed under the weight of our crisis as we experience that great sobering feeling of finitude. In that moment of pause, we re-assess our entire lives, coming to the conclusion that we are bound by our humanity. However, in accepting our finitude, Becker says, as he quotes the great Existentialists Jose Ortega y Gasset and Soren Kierkegaard, that we become truly human, living on the boundary between the immanent and transcendent nature of God.[37] In doing so, we develop a new understanding of God's omnipotence, His ability to interact in the world. We come to understand what Paul Tillich was talking about when he writes that God is not always the deity that splits seas and rains down hail from the heavens; oftentimes, He seems not to be present, yet we feel His presence incarnationally.[38] In the midst of crisis, God becomes very real, although we are often unaware of His presence because we are waiting for a miracle to occur. Yet, most times, God reveals Himself through a friend's embrace or we hear His words through a minister's prayer. In doing so, our prayer is answered, although not in the way that we had expected. In Psalm 30, there is an expectation that God will be faithful to relieve the poet's suffering because it has happened previously. Thus, we realize that deliverance comes, even if the trouble remains.

---

[36] Ernest Becker, *The Denial of Death* (New York: Free Press/Simon and Schuster, 1973), 58-64.

[37] Ibid., 75-82.

[38] Paul Tillich, *Systematic Theology, volume 1* (Chicago: University of Chicago Press, 1951), 204-210 and 279-286.

## DEFINING CRISIS

How exactly do we define "crisis?" If we peruse any number of textbooks on the subject of crisis counseling or crisis ministry, we will find a number of definitions. Some are as simple as Carkhuff and Berenson's definition: "Crisis is a crisis because the individual knows no response to deal with a situation."[39] And there are some that are a little more in-depth, such as this theological definition provided by Charles Gerkin: "A crisis situation is, for modern persons, an extreme or boundary situation in which the fundamental contradiction between human aspirations and finite possibilities becomes visible in such a way as to demand attention."[40] However, the one I like the best comes from Richard James, who teaches counseling at the University of Memphis. He says that a "crisis is a perception or experiencing of an event or situation as an intolerable difficulty that exceeds the person's current resources and coping mechanisms."[41] I think the reason why I like this definition is because it resonates with my experience of helping people in crisis—someone finds himself or herself in the middle of a situation that is so overwhelming that they feel helpless to react to the situation. I received a call from the Emergency Department informing that that a pediatric cardiac arrest was coming in. Now, this is a stressful event for everyone. The ambulance arrived and the EMS crew rushed the baby into the awaiting trauma room. The parents followed close behind, and I escorted them to a quiet room where they would await the outcome. Their reactions were as I had seen before—the ringing of hands, the pacing and rocking, the inability to make phone calls. They were unprepared for this situation and for its sad outcome.

What is critically important to remember is that crisis is a natural part of life; it is what balances out the good that we experience so that we do not forget our place in the universe. Crisis keeps us humble, keeps us dependent on God. According to Howard Stone, there are two types

---

[39] Robert R. Carkhuff and Bernard G. Berenson, *Beyond Counseling and Therapy*, 2nd ed. (New York: Holt, Rinehart and Winston, 1977), 165.
[40] Charles V. Gerkin, *Crisis Experience in Modern Life: Theory and Theology for Pastoral Care* (Nashville: Abingdon, 1979), 32.
[41] Richard K. James, *Crisis Intervention Strategies*, 6th ed. (Belmont, CA: Thomson Higher Education/Brooks-Cole, 2008), 3.

of crisis—developmental and situational.[42] A developmental crisis is an event that everyone will experience, such as the emotional turmoil that is consistent with the adolescent years or the awareness of fragility that is consistent with the later years. A situational crisis, such as the loss of a job or the death of a loved one through a traumatic accident, is unpredictable, chaotic, and random. Their immediate result is often emotionally crippling, as we become profoundly aware that life as we know it has changed. It often takes a great deal of time to process these experiences, as the effects may last for years following the event (i.e., living with PTSD or HIV).

It is difficult to predict how someone will react to a crisis. I have found that everyone has a certain way that they react to a particular crisis. My typical reaction is to hunker down emotionally, to remain level-headed although I may be erupting on the inside. My daughter's reaction is to dive head-long into hysterics. Now, granted she is only six years old. Yet, I have seen similar reactions out of adults that could rival my dramatic daughter. I remember one particular situation when I was called to the OR waiting area. The doctors had just informed a woman that her husband had died during a routine surgery. When I arrived, the place was in pandemonium. What struck me the most was how the man's two daughters reacted. One daughter was very tearful and vocal in her grief, while the other daughter sat stoically and only allowing a thin layer of tears to come from her eyes. When the family finally decided to leave (after the minister preached the man's funeral—TWICE!), the one daughter who had been very emotional had calmed down some and was able to help her mother walk away from the hospital. However, the daughter who had been stoic throughout remained so. My hope was that she would allow herself to fully grieve at some point.

## HOW A CRISIS DEVELOPS

We have identified what a crisis is. It is a situation that stretches us beyond our normal coping limits. Yet, how does a crisis develop? How can we know when we are reaching our limits and entering into a crisis

---

[42] Howard W. Stone, *Crisis Counseling*, 3rd ed., Creative Pastoral Care and Counseling Series (Minneapolis: Fortress, 2009), 3-4.

situation? The following diagram, developed by Howard Stone, provides a simple explanation for a difficult situation:[43]

## PRECIPITATING EVENT→ APPRAISAL→ RESOURCES AND COPING METHODS→ CRISIS

The first stage of Howard's approach is the "precipitating event" stage. It is here that something happens to us that stimulates us to feel threatened, whether it be physically, emotionally, or even spiritually threatened. Examples of these kinds of threats include having a loved one involved in an accident, experiencing a death or divorce, or losing a job. (Although I will say more about this later, it is important to note that there is a difference between trauma and crisis. A trauma is an external event that happens to someone [i.e., being involved in a car accident]. Unless we are involved in the accident, *we do not experience the trauma*, although we experience a crisis due to the trauma. This is an important concept to remember when we are working with family members who find themselves at the hospital because their loved one has been in an accident.) It is also possible to experience spiritual forms of crisis, such as public condemnation or ostracizing due to differing beliefs within a congregation. Boyd Purcell says that spiritual abuse—what he calls "spiritual terrorism"—occurs when ministers, church leaders, and other Christians focus on a "legalistic interpretation of the Holy Bible" and proclaim "mixed messages of God's love and justice."[44]

When we experience some form of threat, we begin assessing the level of danger that this threat brings. This is the second stage—the "appraisal" stage. In order for this event to be a crisis, we must feel that we are in some way in danger. By danger, I mean that the event may radically alter our lives. The separation brought on by death threatens our very sanity because of the loss of companionship; the

---

[43] Ibid., 10.

[44] Boyd C. Purcell, *Spiritual Terrorism: Spiritual Abuse from the Womb to the Tomb* (Bloomington, IN: AuthorHouse, 2008), 3. For more on this concept of spiritual abuse, see David Johnson and Jeff van Vonderen, *The Subtle Power of Spiritual Abuse: Recognizing and Escaping Spiritual Manipulation and False Spiritual Authority Within the Church* (Minneapolis: Bethany House Publishers, 1991); and Marc DuPont, *Toxic Churches: Restoration from Spiritual Abuse* (Grand Rapids, MI: Chosen Books/ Baker, 2004).

loss of a job threatens our security because we may become dependent on an unstable welfare system for support until a new position can be found. This then leads us to the third stage of Howard's approach—the "resources and coping methods" stage. In this stage, we begin to process what resources we have in order to counteract this threat. Resources range from friends and family members to communication skills to financial reserves. If the person's coping mechanisms are effective in managing the threat, then the crisis is adverted. However, if the person's resources are not effective, then the person enters into a true crisis state. This, then, becomes the fourth and final stage of the process—the "crisis" stage. Yet, it is important to remember that the threatening event is only perceived as a crisis to us because we are not able to readily respond to it. *The event in and of itself is not a crisis*; it is our ineffective response to the event that makes it a crisis.

What are some characteristics of a crisis? To answer this question, we turn again to the writing of Richard James. James describes the following as characteristics that define a threatening situation as a crisis.[45] First, there is a *presence of both danger and opportunity*. James says that a crisis is a danger because of the overwhelming nature of the situation. We are pushed well beyond our comfort zones and may lose control of ourselves in the process. Yet, James says that a crisis is also an opportunity because the pain we experience forces us to seek out help.

Second, there is a *complicated symptomology*. It becomes difficult to accurately diagnosis the real threat when we reach our crisis point. In emergency medical care, physicians look for the one problem that brought the patient into the hospital. I have heard doctors talk with patients and, after hearing all that is wrong with them, ask them plainly, "Yes, but what is the problem that caused you to come in tonight?" Diagnosing symptoms is even more taxing in a community crisis, such as in Hurricane Katrina, because there were so many independent contexts that were been pulled together into one inflated crisis.

Third, there are *seeds of growth and change*. In every system, there is a natural reaction against change. Change brings about pain, something that functional people are not comfortable with. Edwin Friedman says that people only change when the pain of staying the same is greater than

---

[45] James, *Crisis Intervention Strategies*, 3-5.

the pain of changing.[46] This is where anxiety comes into play. When our anxiety level peaks, then our body reacts instinctively towards growth and healing.

Fourth, there are no *panaceas or quick fixes*. Much of what I have done as a chaplain and as a minister would fall under the category of "brief therapy" or "solution-focused counseling." In this form of intervention, an immediate problem is resolved with an immediate solution. However, not all crises can be solved immediately. Substance abuse cannot be defeated with a quick fix; yet it is still a crisis that needs to be answered. A true crisis is one that does not have an easy way out.

Fifth, there is *the necessity of choice*. The old axiom of choosing not to choose is a choice is very true in crisis. A perfect example is the spouse who must decide whether or not to take his or her partner off of life-support. In instance after instance, I have seen spouses who cannot accept the reality of the situation and make the change that needs to be made to "allow nature to takes its course," thus inflicting more pain upon themselves and their lover (Yes, I am a proponent of DNR orders in these types of situations. We will get to this in our section on ethics.) Their decision not to choose becomes the choice that they must live with for the rest of their lives. It is when we choose to do something in that moment of crisis that plants the seeds of growth and change into our souls and allows us to confront the crisis positively.

Finally, there are the concepts of *universality and idiosyncrasy*. Everyone will experience a crisis in their lives (the principle of universality). Not everyone will respond to the same crisis in the same way (the principle of idiosyncrasy). Crisis is just like that. In the end, crisis is a part of life. We can choose either to deny this or accept this. If we choose to deny the presence of crisis in our lives, then we will live in anxious paranoia, always afraid of what might happen. If we choose to accept the presence of crisis in our lives, then we will share the expectant faith of the poet who, even in the midst of his own crisis, wrote, "You have turned for me my mourning into dancing; You have loosed my sackcloth and girded me with gladness, That my soul may sing praise to You and not be silent. O LORD my God, I will give thanks to You forever" (Psalm 30:11-12).

---

[46] Edwin H. Friedman, *Generation to Generation: Family Process in Church and Synagogue*, Guilford Family Therapy Series (New York: The Guilford Press, 1985), 47-48.

## CHAPTER 6

# CRISIS INTERVENTION AND REFERRAL

In this chapter, we are going to look at the standard approach to crisis intervention. The proposed approach to crisis intervention is general in nature, and has been generally accepted in practice since it was developed by psychiatrist Warren L. Jones in 1968.[47] It should be noted that this method has been tweaked by pastoral care scholars (primarily Howard Clinebell, Howard W. Stone and David Switzer) to include a "D" component, something that is incredibly important to the congregational minister. Our chapter will conclude will a brief discussion on the process of referral because it is important for ministers to understand that it perfectly acceptable to not have all the answers and be willing to seek out those who can better serve our people.

## KNOWING YOUR HOSPITALS

I spent four years working as a hospital chaplain in a Level-II trauma center. Perhaps this would be the appropriate moment to talk about hospital classification. According to the website for the American College of Surgeons, [48] a Level-I trauma center is a hospital that can provide the highest quality of care to an acutely injured patient. Surgeons from various disciplines stand ready in-house twenty-four hours a day to provide life-saving interventions, and critical care units are staffed with highly-trained, nationally-certified nurses. These hospitals can be all-encompassing centers like the famous Cedars-Sinai

---

[47] Warren L. Jones, "The A-B-C Method of Crisis Management," *Mental Hygiene* 52 (January 1968): 87-89.

[48] http://www.facs.org/trauma/verified.html; accessed 11 June 2012.

Medical Center in Los Angeles or the Duke University Medical Center in Durham, North Carolina. Or it could be a dedicated pediatric facility like the Arkansas Children's Hospital in Little Rock or Cincinnati Children's Hospital.

A Level-II trauma center is still a facility that offers a high quality of care, however it may not be able to meet every medical need. For example, in Huntington, West Virginia, there are two Level-II trauma centers. Both hospitals have twenty-four surgery protocols, although certain specialists stay on-call rather than remain in-house. Both hospitals are serviced by trauma teams from the local university's school of medicine, rotating primary care each day. Both hospitals share transportation services, including a helicopter that can transport a patient to the other hospital in a matter of minutes. However, each hospital, due to state laws, can only provide specialized care in certain medical services. Neither hospital can monopolize medical care in the area. Cabell Huntington Hospital specializes in burn, pediatric and orthopedic care, while St. Mary's Medical Center specializes in cardiac, vascular and stroke care. There have been numerous instances where a patient was brought into one facility for a particular injury only to discover that he or she needed to be transferred to the other facility for additional care.

A Level-III trauma center is generally a rural or community hospital that has a working relationship with the larger, more equipped Level-I or Level-II facilities. They can provide care to critically-injured patients; however their range of care is limited. Examples include the Community Medical Center of Missoula, Montana, and the Poudre Valley Hospital in Fort Collins, Colorado.

A Level-IV trauma center can generally evaluate and stabilize critically-injured patients so that they can be transferred to a higher level of care at another facility. These facilities are required to have trauma-trained staff available; however their ability to offer an immediate intervention may vary.

A Level-V trauma center differs from a Level-IV center in that it may not be open twenty-four hours. Medical facilities in resort areas often fall under this classification as staffing and funding concerns are always an issue. It is important, then, for a minister to determine what types of facilities are in the area, how they cooperate with one another, and where patients go if they are transferred out. This will allow the minister to effectively care for members during traumatic situations.

## ADVANTAGES OF CRISIS INTERVENTION

And speaking of ministering to members during traumatic situations, we will now turn our attention to the standard method of crisis intervention that I mentioned above. Distinguished pastoral care scholar Howard W. Stone notes five advantages that crisis intervention has over a more traditional form of pastoral counseling.[49] First, *crisis intervention is designed to be used only in crisis situations, not in traditional pastoral care situations.* I have a saying: "Not everything is a crisis." There will be times when the A-B-C-D method is pertinent to a pastoral care situation, such as when a family has been involved in a car accident and taken to the emergency room. And there will be times when it is not pertinent to the situation, such as guiding a college student on what summer job he or she should take.

Second, *crisis intervention is a short-term method of pastoral care, therefore the goal is solving an immediate problem.* In-depth pastoral counseling, even when using Carl Roger's person-centered approach, can stir up some bad stuff between the minister and the member. During a counseling session with a man who was hoping to stave off an impending divorce, something in our conversation caused the man to storm out of my office and drive off. He returned the next week and apologized. Yet in a crisis situation, the problem is the focus.

Third, *crisis intervention is applicable to people from all different types of backgrounds.* It is funny how crisis breaks down barriers and reminds us that we are all human before our Creator. It is during a crisis that our defenses come down as we seek immediate solace and comfort from wherever we can find it. I was covering the hospital one Sunday morning when I received a call to the Pediatric ICU. It was not necessarily an emergency in the terms that someone was dying. Yet there was a family with a sick newborn, and they had requested a chaplain to pray with them. The funny thing was that they were expecting a Catholic chaplain, for they asked me "to pray the 'Our Father.'" I modestly informed them that I was not Catholic, to which one of the grandfathers replied, "Well, you're Christian right?" I affirmed that I was, and he

---

[49] Howard W. Stone, *Crisis Counseling*, 3rd ed., Creative Pastoral Care and Counseling Series (Minneapolis: Fortress, 2009), 26.

simply said, "Well, son, pray one of your prayers. I don't think God is going to care right now."

Fourth, *crisis intervention is not a long-term process.* Whereas traditional counseling can take weeks (my basic approach to premarital counseling is twelve weeks) or longer (mentoring can last for years), crisis ministry is intended to last from a few minutes to just a few weeks. Most of my experience consists of ministering to people in crisis during the span of a few hours. However, as any congregational minister knows, ministry in times of mourning does not cease at the funeral. As we will note in our section in the chapters on ministering in times of death, our ministry can usually last up to six weeks following the initial crisis.

And fifth, *crisis intervention is a form of pastoral care that any Christian can practice.* Although some training should be required for those who wish to provide pastoral care, it does not take specialized training to pray at someone's bedside, to hold a box of tissues or to help someone make a phone call. The cover of Kenneth Haugk's little classic *Christian Caregiving: A Way of Life* displays this beautifully—there is the hand of one Christian holding the hand of a hospitalized Christian. Just like in the story of the Good Samaritan, any Christian can offer a cup of cold water, a prayer or a ride to the hospital.

However, as helpful as these concepts are, they cannot guarantee us success when we enter a crisis situation. That is part of crisis theory—we have no idea how the situation is going to turn out. It may turn out the way we hope, or it may turn pear-shaped with weeping and gnashing of teeth. There is just no way to be sure. Therefore, it is important for us to ask ourselves some questions before we enter a crisis situation. First, *why am I getting involved in this situation?* The answer to that question is easy for those of us who are ministers or pastoral care leaders: it is part of our job! However, what if we find ourselves in a domestic dispute or a hostage situation? We must consider carefully our motives for getting involved in any crisis situation.

Second, *are we willing to accept failure as a possible outcome?* When my kids were younger, we took them to see a movie. As we were leaving the theatre, my daughter realized that she had dropped her pacifier. (I will let this horrifying thought wash over all parents.) I went back and searched where we had been sitting until I found the prodigal. It is a trivial example, I know, yet I think that it gives us some perspective on our involvement in crisis situations. Just as I could have come back empty-handed from my pacifier search, there is the very real possibility that our advice could go unheeded, could be misinterpreted, or could simply be wrong. When dealing with people, failure is always a possibility.

Third, *are we aware of the expectations that the person we are ministering to has for us and our position?* From my experience, my presence with a family usually means one of two things—either the person has died or my prayer will resolve the situation. I can honestly say that neither is true every time. There have been times when I met a family to be the emotional buffer before the doctor gives the bad news. Yet there have been plenty of times when meeting the family in the ER lobby was simply protocol.

Fourth, *are we prepared to receive negatively-motivated emotions from those we are ministering to?* Working in an emergency room can be taxing emotionally. I have been accused of keeping family members from their loved ones and blamed for patients dying. There was an instance when the grandmother of a small child let everyone in the emergency room know that I was "a nobody" and that she "didn't have to listen to" me when I asked her to step outside of the room where her grandchild was being treated. I have been threatened with physical violence and even had a weapon pulled on me more than once. While these were difficult situations, they do not match the time that a member of a congregation blamed me for her mother passing away because I "didn't pray hard enough for her to get well." It is in these moments that we must lean on the Lord for strength (Proverbs 3:5). However, once we have asked ourselves these questions and have found our answers satisfactory, then we can engage in the following method of crisis intervention.

## THE A-B-C-D OF CRISIS INTERVENTION

Now, I know what some of you may be thinking at this point: *Wow, this is a lot of information to take in! How could I possibly remember any of this in an actual crisis?* First, I believe that, if you have a calling to ministry, then you also have the power of the Spirit working within you. Remember these words from Paul: "For God has not given us a spirit of timidity, but of power and love and discipline" (2 Timothy 1:7). Training and experience are essential ingredients to good ministry, yet never forget that God will be with you as you minister in these troublesome situations. Also, you may find it helpful to put the "A-B-C-D"s down on a laminated card and carry it with you in your wallet (or you could store it as a text file on your phone).

As I mentioned above, the original approach was developed by Warren Jones and has been tweaked by pastoral scholars and counseling professionals several times since. However the main components have remained the same.[50]

*Achieve contact with the person.* This can be either the person involved in the accident (the one experiencing both the trauma and the crisis) or the family member who has called for your assistance (the one or ones experiencing the crisis). Regardless of who we make contact with, there are four things that will help us begin the intervention process. First, build (or deepen) the relationship by listening carefully and reserving judgment about the situation. Remember, we are there for them, not to satisfy our own agenda. Second, enhance our relationship by using attending, listening, and empathetic actions. These can include but are not limited to praying for them, holding their hands, making phone calls, advocating on their behalf with the medical staff, or giving them a shoulder to cry on. Third, affirm and encourage the person often. During a crisis, it is common for patients or family members to lament about their ability to endure this crisis. There is not time or space to go into the various motives and personality elements that play into this, yet it is important to remind them that they can and will endure this crisis, especially if they are *not* the patient. Occasionally, someone does find it difficult to endure, such as the one instance when a family member began having chest pains and shortness of breath after hearing that her loved one had died. Yet, this is actually quite rare. Fourth, guide the one you are ministering to onto the decision-making path, yet do not make any decisions for him or her. Especially when the crisis is a death, there are numerous decisions that will need to be made. Shock is the body's natural defense mechanism to help us cope with these situations. However many people, without guidance, will repress the natural endorphins that our body provides, thus sacrificing action for apathy and numbness. We must not allow this to happen.

*Boil down the problem to its essential parts.* In a crisis, everything is hyped up and every problem can be a disaster waiting to happen. I

---

[50] I also would recommend a thorough reading of Howard Stone's little book *Crisis Counseling*, if possible, before engaging in any form of crisis ministry.

have seen my fair share of cell phones smashed against walls or down on floors because a call was dropped or reception was not great. In this stage of the intervention process, our goal is to help the person we are ministering to sort out the problems they can solve from the problems they cannot solve. It is amazing how deciding which funeral home to call can make a person in crisis feel productive. Even declining organ donation, regardless of how we may feel about it, can help lift a person out of the chaos of the moment simply because he or she made a decision. This stage, then, has three steps: First, guide the person in deciding which problem to solve first. For example, a middle-aged woman in your congregation has called you and stated that her elderly father has died at the hospital. This family is new to your congregation. Her problem is now two-fold because her father has died and she lacks the resources to make necessary decisions. Her father's death is a problem that she cannot solve, yet she can solve the problem of who to contact for the funeral. She is filled with questions, so your objective is to help her focus on whom to call first. Second, reflect with the person on how he or she has tried to solve this problem. Back to our example: the woman managed the arrangements for her mother because she knew exactly who to call. However, she had previously lived several states away. Although the arrangements are for her mother and father to be buried together, it would be at least a couple of days before the body could be picked up. She knows what she wants to do, yet she does not know how to go about it. This leads us to the last step: guide the person through the process of developing options and assessing resources. Most hospitals have a morgue where bodies can be kept until a funeral home attendant arrives. That is a viable option. Also, a member of your congregation operates a mortuary and has provided a holding service in the past for similar situations. Again, this is another viable option. The only question, then, is which option to choose. Now, what seemed like an unsolvable problem now has two viable solutions.

_Commit to a plan of action._ This is the stage of the intervention process when a decision is made. The wonderful thing about this process is that it can be applied to almost any crisis situation. In our example, we help the young woman develop a plan: she will contact the mortuary back home, leaving the body with the hospital morgue until it can be picked up. Naturally, questions of how long to wait and when to plan the service will begin to flood her mind. Do not dismiss those questions, yet remind her that this is not the time to discuss those questions. She needs to enact her plan so that everything can get started. In another example, we may be working with a husband who has been concealing an alcoholic wife. However, he can no longer hide the emotional and physical signs of abuse and addiction. The plan of action here may be creating a confrontation where his wife is faced with the reality of how her addiction is destroying her life and her family. It is in situations like this that we must be prepared to address any resistance with compassion and commit to not making any decisions or engaging in any actions that the person is capable of making on his or her own.

*Develop a plan for continued care.* Again, staying in contact is incredibly important. As the Scottish poet Robert Burns once wrote, "The best laid schemes o' mice an' men/Gang aft agley" (or, "The best laid plans of mice and men/Often go awry."). Just because a plan was developed does not mean that the plan will work. We will need to assess the effectiveness of the action plan, as well as guide them in developing continued goals by asking "What is the next step?" In the case of the husband seeking help for his wife who is struggling with alcoholism, this may include admittance to a treatment facility for her, a peer group for him, and counseling for any children. Encourage the person to seek assistance from and to seek to assist other who are experiencing or have experienced a similar crisis. Those who have endured a crisis are often the best crisis counselors. Also, help the person find additional resources in order to strengthen their coping strategies. There are several ways that we can engage in continued care of those who are experiencing crisis. For example, we can visit them at home, keep in contact through electronic messaging or phone calls, or connecting them with a support group. Another way we can do this is through referring them to someone more suited or better qualified to help them through the crisis.

## REFERRAL

I can remember one time when the janitor brought someone to my door who was seeking counseling for substance abuse and divorce. As I talked with her, I guessed that I could counsel her about moving on from a divorce, yet I was unsure how to counsel someone who was struggling with drug addiction. I had the contact information for a local Christian counselor who lived on the next block over. It was after hours, so I offered to pray with her and contact the counselor so she would be expecting this woman. She agreed to withdraw from using any form of drugs or drinking any alcohol until she met with the counselor. I also gave her my contact number in case she began going through withdrawal and needed medical attention. I received a phone call from the counselor a few days later thanking me for the referral and said that the woman had committed to counseling and straightening out her life. I also received a reprimand from my leadership because they did not understand why I referred this situation. "You're the minister," they chastised. "What more could this counselor—Christian or not—do for her that you could not?" Since that time, I have learned the benefit of professional ministry—I have limits and it is irresponsible and unethical of me to counsel or minister outside of my competencies. As Gary Collins writes, "Referral does not mean, necessarily, that the original counselor is incompetent or trying to get rid of the counselee. No one person is skilled enough to counsel everyone, and referral is often a way to show your desire to have the counselee get the best help possible."[51] This is not a cop-out. It is me being honest with myself, something that all church leaders should and must be.

In order to be effective in referring those seeking help to the correct agencies or individuals, we must make ourselves familiar with the resources in our communities and we must maintain connections to them. Since most professional individuals, such as therapists and doctors, are bound to tightly-crafted work schedules and case loads, it would be best to make the initial contact through a phone call or email. These contacts will generally be handled by secretaries or receptionists, yet the contact has been made. Most professional agencies also have websites that will detail current information in terms of services provided, rates for compensation or insurance reimbursement, and contact information. Keeping a current list handy by your phone or in your wallet would be wise. When I was a pediatric chaplain, I would carry a small notebook with me that contained all of my daily visit information as well as some other contact information, including the pastoral care or social work offices of hospitals that we would occasionally transfer patients to for additional services. The approach that I used, I think, can also be of

---

[51] Gary R. Collins, *Christian Counseling: A Comprehensive Guide*, rev. ed. (Dallas: Word, 1988), 70.

value to the congregational minister who needs to refer someone to more specialized care. First, contact the referred agency to assess availability. In terms of a counseling situation, the counselor you contact may have a full case load. However he or she may be able to refer your situation to someone else in their practice or to another practice that is not as swamped. Second, once contact has been made, inform the person you are ministering to with the reason for the referral. This may, honestly, be outside your scope of experience and training. Transference, or the "transfer [of] feelings about a person in the past to a person in the present," may have occurred.[52] If this happens, you must transfer the person to another's care. Whatever the reason, let him or her know why you are recommending this course of action. Third, provide the person with contact information, yet allow them to make the appointment. Since you have already contacted the referral agency, *your* responsibility has come to an end. Now it is up to them to seek the help they need. Fourth, provide appropriate information to the referral agency per informed consent from the person you are ministering to. Professional agencies have legally-binding consent forms that must be filled out (and sometimes notarized) before they will accept new patients or their files. In the case of ministers, a letter typed on church letterhead should be adequate. Fifth, stay in contact with the person, especially if he or she is a member of your congregation. Your counseling may be over, however you are still the minister. That being said, it is important to note that ministers should never refer situations that are theological or spiritual in nature because there are no better experts in religion than ministers.[53] If we feel inadequate, then we should seek out further training by studying that issue more deeply, contacting a professor, or asking for instruction from another minister.

---

[52] *Ibid*, 177.
[53] For a helpful, albeit dated, guide, see Robert L. Mason, Jr., Carol B. Currier, and John R. Curtis, *The Clergyman and the Psychiatrist: When to Refer* (Chicago: Nelson-Hall, 1978).

## CHAPTER 7

# FORGIVENESS AND GRIEF

## FORGIVENESS

To be honest, forgiveness is tricky. It is not in our nature as humans to freely offer forgiveness to those who hurt us. It is more in our nature to hold on to the inflicted pain and build up a barrier between ourselves and the one who has injured us. However, to release the pain is to practice mercy and create community. Thus, we are called by our faith to forgive: "[B]earing with one another, and forgiving each other, whoever has a complaint against anyone; just as the Lord forgave you, so also should you" (Colossians 3:13). In addition, Jesus, in His liturgical prayer, teaches that forgiveness is a practice in reciprocity: "And forgive us our debts, as we also have forgiven our debtors" (Matthew 6:12). He emphasizes the importance of the dual practice of forgiveness a couple of verses later when He says that when we forgive, then we will be forgiven (v. 14). Yet, it is also important to accept that if we do not forgive others, then we will not receive the forgiveness of others (v. 15). As Tom Long notes,

> Forgiveness is not a matter of bookkeeping; it is part of a living relationship with God and others. Forgiveness is not a matter of some distant diving accountant burning the note on our sinful debts and saying, "Well, that's that." Forgiveness is to the Christian life like breathing; constant and life-giving. What we breathe in from God's mercy we express to others. Inhale. Exhale. Forgive us, as we forgive; as we forgive, forgive us.[54]

---

[54] Thomas G. Long, *Matthew*, Westminster Bible Companion (Louisville: Westminster/John Knox Press, 1997), 71.

Forgiveness brings about freedom. Freedom from what, you may ask? Freedom from spiritual oppression. Notice that I did not say the forgiveness is freedom from guilt. I can remember a time when I was much younger when I broke a plate and tossed the shattered pieces in the trashcan in order to hide the crime from my parents. However, being young and inexperienced in matters of deception, I did not cover up the pieces. Later in the evening, when my mother saw the broken pieces in the trashcan, she asked me about it. I had been avoiding my parents because of the guilt that I felt. Until the violation was voiced and recompense was made, there was an unsettling aura between my parents and me. Once my mother asked me about it and told me not to worry about it, there was a sense of relief in my soul. Now I know this may seem like an aggrandized story, yet it notes the guilt that all of us are familiar with—what Scott Peck calls *existential guilt.* According to Peck, we need a certain amount of existential guilt to be reminded of our need for God so that we can function appropriately in society.[55] However, if we allow our souls to become burdened with too much guilt, then it becomes *neurotic guilt.*[56] This happens when we do not allow ourselves to feel forgiven. Ironically, according to Peck, Christians suffer more from neurotic guilt because Christians refuse to allow themselves to be forgiven.

Someone once said that forgiveness is giving up our wish for a better past. Most of us have heard that we should "forgive and forget." However, if you have ever tried this, you realize that we cannot "forgive and forget." When we have been hurt, we always remember it. After all, pain is how we know that we are alive. Thus, we can only forgive the pain, remember the pain, and *grow* through the pain. There are three myths about forgiveness that we need to dispel. First, as has already been mentioned, *we cannot forget.* The only way that we can forget the pain would be to have a frontal lobotomy. Second, *we cannot forgive for others.* When we work in the "ministry of reconciliation," we are working to bring two fractured parties together. However, they must make the decision to forgive one another. We can do nothing except serve as an

---

[55] M. Scott Peck, *Further Along the Road Less Traveled: The Unending Journey Towards Spiritual Growth* (New York: Touchstone/Simon and Schuster, 1993), 21.

[56] Ibid., 22.

intermediary. Third, *we cannot forgive ourselves*. Only God can forgive us; all we can do is accept the forgiveness that is offered to us.

Forgiveness is about healing the hurt that we *do not* deserve! Deep hurt flows from a dead past into a living present. We find that these hurts do not go away and we wind up spending all of our time nursing them. Forgiveness is love's toughest work. As Fritz Perls once said that we can never grow up until we are finished with our resentments.[57] However, if not practiced appropriately, we become insufferable manipulators, causing more damage than is necessary. Forgiveness helps us see people for who they are and not how we want to see them. It also helps us see ourselves for who we are and not for whom we want to see ourselves.

> Our "salvation" or our healing does not come in our strivings to rise above what we are or what other men are. Our own ladders by which we climb are only an attempt to disown the shameful or unacceptable side of the self. . . .In some sense, then, the cross is a pushing of all men into a great commonality. None can claim blessing for himself in his own right. Blessing does not come from good works or great heritage. Yet no man wants to start from nothing. The pious man resents being leveled with the prostitute, and the rich protests being the brother of the poor. The cross will not let us live in peace and wholeness unless we affirm there that we are brother of all the broken ones.[58]

We cannot heal the past; we can only grow through our pain. When we offer forgiveness, we change and we begin to see the world differently.

Yet, simply offering forgiveness to someone who hurt us undeservedly is difficult. Lewis Smedes (1921-2002), in his ironically titled book *Forgive and Forget* (this was actually *not* what he had titled it), developed a four-stage process to forgiveness that works similarly to Elisabeth

---

[57] Frederick S. Perls, *Gestalt Therapy Verbatim* (Reprint: 1969. Gouldsboro, ME: Gestalt Journal Press, Inc., 1992), 68.
[58] Myron C. Madden, *The Power to Bless: Healing and Wholeness through Understanding* (Nashville: Broadman Press, 1970), 154-155.

Kubler-Ross' stages of grief (which we will discuss below).[59] First, there is the *hurt* stage. In this stage, someone causes us (unfair) pain and we find ourselves unable to forget it. People hurt us for a variety of reasons, some of them intentional and some of them unintentional. Yet, regardless of the reason, we have been inflicted with needless pain. Second, there is the *hate* stage. We cannot shake the pain we feel and we want them to hurt as we do. I know that some may be uncomfortable with the word "hate." Yet, to use any other word would be to diminish the intensity of the sensation that we feel. I tell my kids, emotions are neither good nor evil—they just are. It is how we react in the moment of our emotion that determines the purity or villainy of our action. God gave us the ability to hate, which allows us to know how much we hurt. Third, there is the *healing* stage. We are able to see the person who hurt us in a new light and become free of our hurt. And fourth, there is the *homecoming* stage. In this stage, we renew our relationship and we accept the person for who they really are—broken, just as we are. It is here when we offer forgiveness to the one who has hurt us or receive forgiveness from the one whom we have hurt. Yet, what if we are unable to speak with the person who hurt us or the person we hurt? What if that person has died? What if that person is out of contact, has moved, changed their name, or refuses to engage us? This is the beauty of forgiveness. Jesus, in the Matthew 6 passage quoted above, does not say that we can only offer and receive forgiveness from those that we can see directly. He simply says to ask forgiveness so that we may be forgiven. Homecoming is not necessary in order to find healing. The simple act of requesting forgiveness or offering forgiveness soothes our spiritual and emotional pain.

Now, you may be wondering to yourself why we are discussing forgiveness in a book about crisis ministry. The reason is that the issue of forgiveness will come up, in some situations. People will speak about hurts that they have or hurts that they have caused. When they do, they are confessing to us. As Purnell encourages us, we should "be present to the other, be alert, and listen without judgment."

> Confessional conversation emerges in the informal and
> unguarded moment when the other person feels safe

---

[59] Lewis B. Smedes, *Forgive and Forget: Healing the Hurts We Don't Deserve* (New York: HarperCollins, 1984), 1-37.

enough to risk revealing the deeply troubling thing. Be alert. Be open. Recognize when people are trying to say something in a different way. Value what they share. Don't judge them. You do not have to approve of the action but you can listen.[60]

I remember visiting a man once on a "routine visit" one weekend while I was on call. As we talked, he informed me that he had served a couple of tours in Vietnam. He began telling me about many of the gruesome things that he had seen and done while serving our country. He asked me, with tears in his eyes, "Do you think God will forgive me for the things that I have done?" "Let's ask Him," was my reply. I prayed for him, asking God not only to forgive him but also to take away the guilt that he felt about what he had done. When the prayer was finished, I saw something that I can only attribute as a touch of the divine—the man expanded, as if a crushing weight had been lifted off of him. He died a few days later. The chaplain that was with him when he died said that he wanted to thank me for hearing his confession and praying for him. In that moment, when guilt becomes more than the person can tolerate, when crisis is only moments away from rearing its ugly head, take a moment and listen. In doing so, we practice "the ministry of reconciliation" by being God's conduit of grace.

## GRIEF

Whereas forgiveness is tricky, grief, as Ian McShane's character Paul Griffin in *We Are Marshall* says, is messy. We often think of grief affecting those who experience the death of a loved one. However, grief is something that we experience whenever we lose anything. In fact, even forgiveness is also an exercise in grief because we must "lose" the pain that has fueled our motives and actions. In grief, we must eventually replace what we have lost with positive energy in order to emotionally, spiritually, and psychologically grow through the loss transition. If we do not, we remain stuck in our grief, unable to cope with life, again fueled with negative energy that stunts our development.

---

[60] Douglas Purnell, *Conversation as Ministry: Stories and Strategies for Confident Caregiving* (Cleveland, OH: The Pilgrim Press, 2003), 138.

There are three primary myths about grief that we will encounter in our ministry to people who have experienced loss. First, there is the myth that says that we do not care if we grieve. Some people will continue living as if their loved one is still very active in their lives. I once counseled an older woman who kept saying that her husband was simply on an extended trip because she could not bear grieving his death. However, letting our loved ones go means putting them in their proper place in our memory. We find ourselves thinking what would he or she do in this situation, or we remember some lesson that he or she taught us that has now proved useful. If we did not care about our loved ones, then we would not remember them. Second, there is the myth that says that our loved ones would not have existed if we grieve them. On the surface, this one makes almost no sense, yet, in the midst of crisis, everything makes sense. This one can be exemplified by Robert de Niro's character Jack Burns in *Meet the Parents*. He keeps his mother's ashes in an urn on his mantle. During dinner, he speaks to his mother's urn as if he were speaking directly to her. When Ben Stiller's character accidently breaks the urn and spills the ashes, Jack acts like his mother has died all over again, only this time she has entered into an existential state of oblivion. Third, there is the myth that says that we do not know how to grieve. *This is a defense mechanism*, and it can be useful for a time. However, there is an innate ability within each of us to grieve. I am not a crier, although I do get choked up when I watch *We Are Marshall*. However, I have grieved losses in my life. It is also important to point out that people will grieve different types of losses differently. Someone may weep openly over the loss of a close family member yet barely shed a tear over the loss of a job. However, when we lose something or someone we are attached to, we will grieve.

Death is the one aspect of life that none of us will escape; it is also the one aspect of life that we will never fully understand. And whenever we experience death, we will also experience grief. There are at least three major paradigms for understanding the grief process. The most popular one was developed by Elisabeth Kubler-Ross (1926-2004), and was originally done within the context of her work with dying patients. The components of her five-stage paradigm include denial ("This cannot be true!"), anger ("It was not a mistake!"), bargaining ("Please, God, take this away!"), depression ("I have no reason to live!"), and acceptance ("I will meet the challenge!").[61] However, the application of her work has been seriously misunderstood. I agree with Richard James' assessment:

> In her five-stage model, Elisabeth Kubler-Ross outlines the human reactions or responses that people experience as they attempt to cope with their own imminent deaths. Her concepts have also been applied to the process of grief and bereavement following most personal loses. The model is a general conceptual framework that does not purport to be applicable in every detail to every person nor to be used in any linear counseling method. Regretfully, it has been used in that manner. . .[62]

The paradigm created by Kubler-Ross is a wonderful paradigm for helping us cognitively understand the process of death and grief. Yet it really does little for helping us understand why people act the way that they do in grief. For the most part, Kubler-Ross' paradigm really is not a paradigm at all. To see it as a paradigm is misleading because there is so much fluidity in the grieving process. It might be more instructive to see these concepts as emotional benchmarks that help shape and define the grieving process, instead of seeing them as signs that someone is moving along at an appropriate pace.

Remember back when I talked about the difference between "being" and "doing" in ministry. For the most part, all of that is still true. However, when working with people who are experiencing a grief crisis, ministry really does become more about "doing" than "being" because the grief process is an emotive and action-oriented process. According to Relational Theory, our attachment to an object (whether person or thing) remains strong as long as we are in connection to that object. When the object is lost (i.e., death of a loved one), we feel a sense of loss. Initially we want to fill the gap left within us; however we will eventually

---

[61] Elisabeth Kubler-Ross lays out her concept in much more extensive detail in chapters 3-7 of *On Death and Dying* (New York: Macmillan). She also modified her paradigm to be applicable to those who experience "living grief," those who mourn the loved and loss; see Elisabeth Kubler-Ross and David Kessler, *On Grief and Grieving: Finding the Meaning of Grief through the Five Stages of Loss* (New York: Scribner, 2005), 7-28.

[62] Richard K. James, *Crisis Intervention Strategies*, 6th ed. (Belmont, CA: Thomson Higher Education/Brooks-Cole, 2008), 365.

discover that we cannot replace that which was lost. Thus, we will only find resolution through altering the significance of the object so that we can make room in our heart/mind/soul for new objects. This is when we appropriately grieve our loss. Here is a simpler way of conceptualizing this approach:

- *Shock*—This is the special stage before we enter into grief.
- *Head*—This is the cognitive stage of grief when we think about and verbalize our grief. In this stage, we hear and recite back the words "he's dead" or "she's dead," yet the emotional connection has yet to be made.
- *Heart*—This is the affective stage of grief when we feel our grief. In this stage, we emote our loss in some way (e.g., crying, being silent, screaming in anger, climbing into the bed with our loved one, etc.).
- *Hands*—This is the connotative stage of grief when we do something. In this stage, we make phone calls to pass along the sad news to others, make funeral arrangements, and try to order our lives accordingly.

We will continue through this cycle several times and at various intensities throughout our lives. We will never completely "get over" the loss. Although, if we process it correctly, our grief will move from being counterproductive to productive over time. The rituals that we will begin to associate with the loss will become a regular part of our lives as we continue to remember the loss. However, we will find ourselves not being so tied to the loss, as it becomes a part of our journey instead of a large blockade on the path.

## CHAPTER 8

# BOUNDAREIS, STRESS, DEPRESSION, BURNOUT

Why are you interested in ministry? Self-help gurus will tell you that you can eliminate stress, thus depression and burnout, from your life. However, *stress is a natural part of life!* The only way to fully eliminate stress is to die. Robert Lutz writes, "I am convinced that many if not most ministers do not take adequate physical and emotional care of themselves"[63] This being said, I feel that now is a good time for a reality check (or two).

*Reality Check # 1—Everyone has co-dependent tendencies!* If you have ever not liked someone yet could not stand to live without them, you have experienced co-dependency. While co-dependency is a dysfunction that plagues some, anyone involved in a relationship is a co-dependent.

*Reality Check # 2—Ministry is co-dependency in action.* Actually, all human services fields (i.e., medicine/nursing, education, therapy, and ministry) are exercises in needing to be needed. If our livelihood is based on being liked, then we are co-dependent. *This is the disease that plagues ministry!*

Co-dependency is resisting life the way it is. It is our denial of who we are and the inability to share ourselves with people. It is a set of symptoms that represses feelings and support compulsive behaviors. Codependency is a disease of extreme and excessive nurturing. It is a lifestyle that was learned in order to survive! While co-dependency

---

[63] Robert R. Lutz, "Surviving in Ministry: A Theological Dilemma," in *Surviving in Ministry: Navigating the Pitfalls, Experiencing the Renewals,* ed. Robert R. Lutz and Bruce T. Taylor (New York/Mahwah, NJ: Integration Press/Paulist Press, 1990), 1.

is *a* problem, it is not *the* problem in ministry and pastoral self-care. However, not realizing and accepting our co-dependent tendency is the beginning of what I call the "BSDB cycle." The cycle of this disease has killed many careers in ministry many times over.

# The "B-S-D-B" Cycle

What does "BSDB" stand for?

- B—Boundaries
- S—Stress
- D—Depression
- B—Burnout

It is important to note that this cycle is a natural, albeit dysfunctional, part of any career or life change that we make.

## B—BOUNDARIES

Boundaries are lines that we draw to help define our roles and interactions in relationships. Established professional boundaries provide a means to protect the space between our power, gained from our professional position, and access to private information about the other's vulnerability. When we exploit our position of power to meet our needs rather than the other's, we have violated our boundaries. Both people in the relationship have to receive something for the relationship to be healthy. Healthy boundaries allow a person to experience comfortable interdependence, resulting in functional relationships.

Boundaries become damaged due to mixed messages and abuse, and they are usually related to family-of-origin issues. There are four types of boundaries—physical, sexual, emotional, and spiritual. These boundaries are interconnected. Physical and sexual abuse leads to emotional and spiritual abuse. We create "walls" when we are hurt by others, thinking these "walls" will protect us in the future. However, these "walls" only create a state of loneliness, and prevent us from establishing trusting and intimate relationships. In ministry, boundaries are either too porous or too impermeable. This is what is known as "boundary blurring."

## S-STRESS

Remember what I mentioned earlier about stress—*stress is a natural part of life.* It is like pain in that it helps remind us that we are alive and that we are dependent upon God's divine action. To tweak Scott Peck's paradigm about guilt that we discussed in the previous chapter, there is "existential" stress (stress that is natural to life, such as relationships and work) and there is "neurotic" stress (stress created by external forces that cause us undue anxiety). Effective ministry is a balancing act between the two types of stress. Charles Rassieur writes, "Simply preaching a sermon is an act that in itself merits praise, but it must be a remarkable sermon before the pastor receives much positive affirmation. And even though the pastor has had an extraordinary week of emergencies expertly handled, there is always something someone can find to criticize"[64]

Our bodies are not geared to deal with stress the way we and others want us to deal with stress. Some are able to thrive on stress, while others buckle under varying amounts of stress. Our society rewards the 16-hour workday (even in ministry) and creates medical reasons for dealing with stress, which is a psychological and spiritual disconnect from our bodies. Again Rassieur writes, "At its worst, ministry can degenerate into the frustrated exercises of a high-achiever who is afraid of rejection, responding anxiously to vague and limitless expressions of need. The pastor assumes that a little more effort will bring the hoped-for praise."[65] When this happens, we engage in a pattern of self-destructive behavior that will eventually cause us and others great anguish.

## D-DEPRESSION

When our "neurotic" stress levels reach critical levels, depression sets in. Depression can affect anyone at anytime, yet we are not talking about clinical depression. We are talking about a type of "emotional distress" that reveals itself as a "sense of 'stuckness' that defines our depression."[66] We open ourselves up to this cycle every time we experience a life-cycle

---

[64] Charles L. Rassieur, *Stress Management for Ministers* (Philadelphia: Westminster Press, 1982), 25.

[65] Ibid., 26.

[66] James S. Gordon, *Unstuck: Your Guide to the Seven-Stage Journey Out of Depression* (New York: Penguin, 2008), 54.

change. As Papolos and Papolos write, "Mood changes are hallmarks of the human experience, and mood has a powerful evolutionary value: it regulates our disposition to action and behavior, and keeps us involved in life and yet relatively safe. . . .An immoderate mood disposition can cause life to be fragmented, disorganized, painful, and potentially dangerous."[67] This, then, helps us distinguish between two types of depression:

- *Exogenous*—Reactive depression or situational transient depression.
- *Endogenous*—Psychotic depression or loss of reality.

Most people experience *exogenous* depression, that sense of not wanting to do anything or a loss of drive.

## B—BURNOUT

Burnout occurs when we continue in our work with people yet have no interest in doing so except for the fact that we do not know what else to do with ourselves.

- Physicians who no longer have good "bedside manner."
- Ministers who hole themselves up in their studies.
- Teachers who do not allow questions or dialogue.

The term "burnout" is perhaps misleading because we are not like rockets that flame out. Thus, it would seem that the therapeutic term "compassion fatigue" is more fitting because we continue in ministry although we no longer know why we are doing so. Stanley Grenz writes, "We risk giving unwarranted significance to our work when we confuse work with productivity."[68] According to Olsen and Grosch, burnout occurs when we get trapped between the "competing feedback loops" of our family system and our congregational system.[69] We get so caught

---

[67] Demitri Papolos and Janice Papolos, *Overcoming Depression*, 3rd ed. (New York: HarperCollins, 1997), 4.

[68] Stanley J. Grenz, "Burnout: The Cause and the Cure for a Christian Malady," *Currents in Theology and Mission* 26 (December 1999): 427.

[69] David C. Olsen and William N. Grosch, "Clergy Burnout: A Self Psychology and Systems Perspective," *Journal for Pastoral Care and Counseling* 45 (Fall 1991): 300-301.

up in meeting the needs of others that we have no time for ourselves. Eventually, we lose all interest in ministering to others and only care about our needs (narcissism).

## MANAGING THE CYCLE

It takes more than saying "no" from time to time. It also takes more than accepting that this cycle is part of life. It takes an intentional effort to reclaim the *practice* of ministry as spirituality in action. As Alasdair MacIntyre writes, "Practice is any coherent and complex form of socially established cooperative human activity through which goods internal to that form of activity are realized."[70] It also means that we, as ministers, must accept that the practice of our calling is about walking the fine line between congregation and home.

Henri Nouwen writes, "Making one's own wounds a source of healing, therefore, does not call for a sharing of superficial personal pains but a constant willingness to see one's own pain and suffering as rising from the depth of the human condition which all men share."[71] The key to is to practice what Edwin Friedman calls *differentiation*:

> Differentiation means the capacity of a family member to define his or her own life's goals and values apart from surrounding togetherness pressures, to say 'I' when others are demanding 'you' and 'we.' It includes the capacity to maintain a (relatively) non-anxious presence in the midst of anxious systems, to take maximum responsibility for one's own destiny and emotional being.[72]

Beyond the practice of differentiation, Eugene Peterson's "angles" of "pastoral integrity" provide useful direction:

---

[70] Alasdair MacIntyre, *After Virtue: A Study in Moral Theory*, 2nd ed. (South Bend, IN: University of Notre Dame Press, 1984), 187.

[71] Henri J. M. Nouwen, *The Wounded Healer: Ministry in Contemporary Society* (New York: Image Books/Doubleday, 1990), 88.

[72] Edwin H. Friedman, *Generation to Generation: Family Process in Church and Synagogue*, Guilford Family Therapy Series (New York: Guilford Press, 1985), 27.

- *Prayer*—Where we take time to listen to God instead of doing all the talking.
- *Scripture Reading*—Where we take time to allow God to speak to us.
- *Spiritual Direction*—Where we enter into a relationship with another traveler in order to speak and be spoken to.[73]

---

[73] Eugene H. Peterson, *Working the Angles: The Shape of Pastoral Integrity* (Grand Rapids, MI: Eerdmans, 1987).

## CHAPTER 9

# ILLNESS AND HOSPITALIZATION

## WHY DO WE BECOME ILL?

Now, here's a $64,000 question if there ever was one. Systems Theory plainly says that when the system becomes dysfunctional, symptoms reveal themselves in order to alert us of the faltering condition. Picture a leaky sink. Not long after we moved into our current house, I noticed that some towels that were kept under the bathroom sink were soaking wet. When I investigated the situation, I discovered that one of the elbow joints had come loose, which was causing water to spew out of the pipe and make quite a mess. The leak was caused by a clog in the pipe. Once I cleaned out the pipe and reassembled everything, the water flowed fine and the leak stopped.

An illness works in much the same way as a leak in a pipe—it lets us know that something in the system is not working properly. A couple of years ago, I woke up one evening with severe pain in my left shoulder and numbness in my left arm. Unable to ease the pain with OTC medication, I went to the Emergency Room. Thankfully, my illness was nothing severe—it was merely a panic attack. I was under a great deal of stress at the time, and this attack was a physical manifestation of how overworked my mind and spirit were at the time. You see, contemporary medical practices can only go so far in treating our illnesses. Take a look at the following figure:

| SYMPTOM | CAUSE |
|---|---|
| Shortness of breath, chest pain | Heart disease |

This is a classic diagnosis. You come to your local emergent care facility or walk-in clinic with the above symptoms, you will most likely be diagnoses with the above cause. In modern medicine—especially in emergent, triage-based care—the goal is to find a physical reason for your illness and treat it efficiently and quickly. At the hospital where I ministered, the ER doctors take all of the tests that are conducted on a patient and funnel them through a diagnostic tool that guides them in deciding what is actually wrong with the patient. They will then prescribe a take-home treatment, return procedure, or admission to treat the condition. Yet, could there be more at play than simply a systematic illness that manifests itself in a set of physical symptoms? Could we attribute our illnesses to something else other than a bad heart?

Malcolm Ballinger believes that there is deeper meaning to our illnesses than we think. In a classic article, Ballinger says that our illnesses are "beloved symptoms" of deeper issues at work.[74] He challenges us to see all illnesses such as heart disease, lung cancer, and AIDS not as the root cause of our medical problems, but to see them as the symptoms of our ill spiritual condition. According to Ballinger, what we commonly call symptoms (such as shortness of breath) are actually physical signs of symptoms that point to a much more important illness than heart disease. Thomas Oden writes, "The roots of our word *health* reflect the wholeness that psychosomatic interface. Health means to have hale or good functioning of both quasi-independent dimensions of human existence: physical and spiritual."[75] Psychosomatic illnesses are illnesses that are more emotional or mental in origin yet present themselves in physical ways (i.e., my panic attack that I mentioned earlier). Roughly half of all hospitalized patients "suffer" from some kind of psychosomatic illness. Ballinger argues that all illnesses, or at least those that are not caused by chaos and fate, are actually psychosomatic because their origin is in our soul.

Ballinger says that there are eight ways to understand illness.[76] First, an illness is a *violation of the laws of health*. There is a reason why I always check the fuel level in my lawn mower before I begin cutting the grass. It ran pretty good for being twenty years old—it is a Craftsman after all—until it suddenly stopped. I made sure that it was not jammed

---

[74] Malcolm B. Ballinger, "The Need for Illness," *Pastoral Psychology* 17 (October 1966): 10.

[75] Thomas C. Oden, *Pastoral Theology: Essentials for Ministry* (New York: HarperCollins, 1983), 261.

[76] Ballinger, "The Need for Illness," 11-17.

with too many clippings and I primed the engine several times. Yet it did not start. Finally, I checked the fuel tank and found that it was empty. A machine cannot run on an empty gas tank. The same is true for us. We make decisions, and those decisions have consequences. If we allow our spiritual gas tank to get low, then it can cause us more than the proverbial headache.

Second, an illness is a *defense against infection, virus, injury, trauma, or other phenomena of the physical universe.* Symptoms let us know that something is wrong with our systems. Ironically, illnesses are generated in order to help our bodies heal.

Third, an illness is a *punishment for sins committed.* Now, it does not matter if we believe this if the patient does. Illness brings forth spiritual concerns that need to be addressed. The writer of Hebrews says this:

> It is for discipline that you endure; God deals with you as with sons; for what son is there whom *his* father does not discipline? But if you are without discipline, of which all have become partakers, then you are illegitimate children and not sons. Furthermore, we had earthly fathers to discipline us, and we respected them; shall we not much rather be subject to the Father of spirits, and live (12:7-9)?

God chastises His children. Yet, does He cause our illnesses? Paul writes that "For the wages of sin is death, but the free gift of God is eternal life in Christ Jesus our Lord" (Romans 6:23), and Moses exhorts the children of Israel to "So choose life in order that you may live, you and your descendants" (Deuteronomy 30:19b). Even the psalmist writes, "When I kept silent about my sin, my body wasted away through my groaning all day long" (32:3). It would seem that there is at least a cursory connection between sin and physical illness. Thus, perhaps we can understand our illnesses as an attempt by our body to purge itself of our sins.

Fourth, an illness *alerts us to an undesirable condition.* Our body is like the guard on the watchtower in Ezekiel 33. Just like a security detail is trained to patrol the land and alert the sentinels of potential threats, our bodies are designed to regulate our systems and alert us when those systems become dysfunctional. We can choose to heed the warnings or ignore the warnings.

Fifth, an illness is a *way of expressing or discharging emotional feelings*. Our culture is not a culture of respect or one that values self-care. We expect too much of ourselves. Thus we inflict a great deal of turmoil upon ourselves and upon our bodies. In many ways, our bodies became our emotional scapegoat (cf., Leviticus 16:20-22). We throw all of our emotional and spiritual garbage onto our bodies, never thinking that our bodies will throw our emotions back at us. Yet, when it does, it is ugly.

Sixth, an illness is an *avoidance of escape from difficult, unwanted, or misunderstood life situations*. If you don't believe me, just ask yourself what caused your headache the next time one comes one.

Seventh, an illness *may prevent God an opportunity to bring about a recuperation or reevaluation of a situation*. Illnesses allow us an opportunity to evaluate our lives and our motives. Illnesses can provide enlightenment and illumination that we may not otherwise be provided.

Eighth, *God needs our illness to handle our creatureliness*. Sanctification is something we work with God on. God does the perfecting, yet we must open our hands and let go of whatever we are holding onto that is preventing God from completing His divine work. In illness, we lose some things. When everything else has been taken away from us, all we have left is God. It is in these times that we become perfected because we finally learn the lesson that God was teaching Paul regarding his health problems: "My grace is sufficient for you, for power is perfected in weakness" (2 Corinthians 12:9). Thus, in our moments of weakness we find our strength as we are reminded that we are dependent upon One greater than us.

## MAKING THE VISIT

As I was preparing this chapter on making visits, I quickly discovered that what Dietrich Bonhoeffer has to say on the importance of the visitation of the sick is probably better than anything that I could conjure up. With regard to the minister's regularity in visiting, Bonhoeffer writes:

> Sick visits should be regular. Bear in mind that they are for the sake of the sick person. People never expect others to show up so much as they do when sick. It is best to schedule the visit in advance so the sick person can get

presentable. Announced visits are more worthwhile than surprise visits. The pastor mustn't ignore a scheduled visit. You can't imagine how much damage you'll do if you don't show up. Scheduling regular visits pledges the pastor to be prepared and the sick person to be ready. If possible, the visits should always be scheduled at the same hour and on the same day of the week.

Regular visits are also good for the pastor. He should be present with the sick often. In such a way he will learn that sickness and health go together. This is not abnormal. Sickness and pain are a law of the fallen world. A person who happens to experience fallenness in this special way is an image of the One who bore our sickness and was so afflicted that people hid their faces from him (Isaiah 53).[77]

I agree with everything Bonhoeffer says, although I should add one caution that he does not. It is important to remember that the hospital's schedule does not revolve around our visiting schedule. As Katie Maxwell reminds us, "Although visitors are usually a welcome relief from the boredom and isolation of the hospital room, be aware that the timing of your visit may not always be met with the enthusiasm you hoped for."[78] There are all kinds of things that can inhibit our visits, including the patient. As in all things, we should always be respectful of the situation and flexible enough to alter our course at the last moment.

It is also important to remember that when we come along the bedside, we do so as the representative of God and a continuation of the Incarnation. We become the intercessor and intermediary between the sick and the Author of Salvation. Thus, we must be ready to hear them in their moment of crisis. Bonhoeffer continues:

> Sick people ask for healing. They cry for release from this body of death into a new and healthy body. They cry for the new world in which "God will wipe away every tear, and there will be no more suffering or crying or pain" (Rev. 21:4). Insofar as this happens, the sick inquire about

---

[77] Dietrich Bonhoeffer, *Spiritual Care*, trans. Jay C. Rochelle (Philadelphia: Fortress Press, 1985), 55-56.

[78] Katie Maxwell, *Bedside Manners: A Practical Guide to Visiting the Ill* (Grand Rapids, MI: Baker, 1990), 29.

Christ more than do the well. Christ fulfills this conscious or unconscious expectation through his promise, "I am the Lord, your physician" (Exodus 15:26).[79]

What is most important is to respect the humanity of the sick. In our technologically-advanced society, it is quite easy to see patients simply as diagnoses or as numbers on an armband. Practitioners so often become callous in their profession, explaining death as a simple process while the family wells up in anguish. Thus, it is important to always keep our "creatureliness" (to use Ballinger's term) before us.

> The sick person must not get the impression that, in his condition, he is unnecessary or useless. . . .Truth belongs at the sickbed. The pastor should never come with cheap and false comfort that life will soon be all right once more. How is he to know that? On the other hand, he shouldn't say that it will soon be all over. He had no certainty of that either. What the sick need to know in any event is that they are special and uniquely lodged in God's hand, and that God is the giver of life whether in this world or the next.[80]

To be honest, there is no one right way to visit someone who is ill. The best advice that I have ever received about visiting the sick is to let the patient be my guide. If he or she is open to a visit, then stay with them as long as necessary to meet their needs. Yet, if they are not interested in a visit, then offer them a blessing and the assurance that we can return, if requested. However, there are some considerations to make before making such a visit. And the first rule of pastoral care is: *always expect the unexpected.* Here are some other tips for making hospital visits:

- **Before You Go:**
    - o Remember that no minister is ever too important to visit someone in the hospital, nursing home or at home. Visitation is essential to effective pastoral ministry.

---

[79] Bonhoeffer, *Spiritual Care*, 56-57.
[80] *Ibid*, 58-59.

- o   Remember that you go to meet the needs of the one you are visiting, not to meet any kind of agenda.
- o   Remember that you are a guest of the facility where the patient is being treated. Be respectful of and thankful for that generosity.
- o   Remember to bring your Bible with you. When I was a chaplain, I would carry a pocket-sized Bible with me. If you have a smartphone, you can download an app that contains several versions (I recommend the YouVersion app).

- •   **While You're There:**
  - o   Check with the unit desk before visiting the patient's room. There may be stipulations regarding visiting the patient that you are unaware of.
  - o   When entering the room, knock loud enough so that they can hear you but not so loud that you would wake them if they are sleeping.
  - o   Practice FIFO ("foam in, foam out"). It helps to prevent the spread of germs and contaminants, and the facility will appreciate your consideration.
  - o   Take a look around the room when you enter. Take note of the patient's condition, especially if any activity is occurring. Also take note of who is there and what their emotional condition is.
  - o   Be careful not to kick the bed when entering or exiting the room.
  - o   Be near the patient so that they can see you without difficulty, but do not sit *on* the bed (pull up a chair or stand at about the level of the patient's waist). Do not do all the talking! Remember that you are there for them. Listen when they talk, and sit in silence when they do not.
  - o   Avoid meaningless and flippant clichés. The hospital room is not the place for sentimentality.
  - o   Avoid the temptation to make them laugh. Humor has its place, yet it must be appropriately times and appropriately delivered. In short, if you are not naturally funny, avoid the compulsion to be so when visiting the sick.

- o Speak loud enough so that the patient can hear you yet not so loud that you can be heard out in the hall.
- o Be careful not to immediately side with the patient against the hospital without talking with both the patient and the patient's care team.
- o Don't overstay your welcome. They know you are busy and they really do appreciate the time you have taken to see them. Also, they *need* their rest.
- o Inform the patient of when you may try to visit again or how they can contact you in between visits.
- o Offer to pray with them.
- o Ask the patient if it is agreeable or appropriate for them to receive visits/calls from other members of the congregation. Most hospitals have published visitation policies. Also, check with the chaplain's office to see what requirements and restrictions are in place regarding religiously-affiliated visitors. Additionally, make sure that you are aware of the current HIPAA policies regarding the release of patient information.

- • **After the Visit:**
  - o To the best of your ability, keep your follow-up appointment!
  - o Remember to visit the patient once they have returned home and check in on them once they are recuperating.

## KEEPING RECORDS

I used to think that it was insulting to be expected to keep records of my visits. And when the purpose of doing so is simply to prove that you are "doing your job," it is insulting. However, I have learned two lessons that are important about keeping records. First, if it is not recorded, then it did not happen. One of the first skills that I was taught during my clinical training was how to fill out the computer record for a pastoral care visit. The chaplain that trained us put it very simply: "If the visit is not recorded, then it did not happen. And if it did not happen, then we don't get paid." On one hand, keeping records is simply a smart practice, especially in a highly litigious society. The ability to produce a verified record is *the* easiest way to navigate a legal conflict. On the other hand, keeping records is the mark of a professional. Cataloging the visit strengthens our listening and perceiving skills. As we strain to remember the visit, our mind will recall elements of the visit, such as the layout of the room, who was present, how the patient communicated with us, etc. The more recording we do, the better we become at picking up these details which leads to an improvement in our practice because we are more attentive. Second, it provides us with a touchstone into people's lives. It provides a narration of the pastoral encounter for future reflection and professional evaluation.[81] It also provides guidance and assistance to others who may be involved in providing pastoral care to the sick.[82] You can find a template for a general "pastoral care note" that I have devised in the Appendix. However, here are the key components of any good record:[83]

- *Patient's vitals*: Name, age, gender, marital status, ethnicity;
- *Visit vitals*: Location, date of visit, time of visit, number of visit(s), reason for visit;
- *Condition of patient*: Do not be technical here. Describe what you see in terms of the condition of the room and what you can physically see regarding the patient. *Do not offer a diagnosis of the patient's condition!*
- *Reactions/responses/comments from the patient*: What did he or she talk about? How are they feeling? What are their concerns?
- *Condition of the family (if present)*: What is their involvement?
- *Reactions/responses/comments from the family (if present)*: What did they talk about? How are they handling the situation?
- *Actions taken by the minister*: What did you do during the visit?
- *Reflection on the visit.*
- *Follow-up and/or Referral Notes (if necessary)*: What is your continued plan of care? What resources need to be directed to the patient?

---

[81] For more guidance on this subject, see Rob A. Ruff, "'Leaving Footprints': The Practice and Benefits of Hospital Chaplains Documenting Pastoral Care Activity in Patients' Medical Records," *Journal of Pastoral Care and Counseling* 50 (Winter 1996): 383-391.

[82] See Louis Nieuwenhuijzen, "Spiritual Care Illustrated: Creating a Shared Language," *Journal of Pastoral Care and Counseling* 61 (Winter 2007): 329-341.

[83] During the editorial process of this manuscript, I came across a wonderful web resource called CareNotebook. To conserve space here, I point you to their website (https://thecarenotebook.com) and my review in the Winter 2015 issue of *Leadership Journal*.

CHAPTER 10

# TRAUMA AND PTSD

## HOW DO WE DEFINE TRAUMA?

In this chapter, we are going to look at the most basic yet also most serious of all of crises—the traumatic situation. My ministry as a chaplain was often dictated by traumas—motor vehicle accidents, shootings, stabbings, falls, and other situations that put a person's life in jeopardy. As I roamed room to room throughout the Emergency Department or wandering from floor to floor in the main hospital, I constantly kept my ears attuned for the announcement that will put everything else on hold: "Trauma Alert. Adult. Priority 2. ETA 5 minutes by ground." It was clear and carefully pronounced, yet it would set the entire hospital in motion. Even more so was the following form of the announcement: "Trauma Alert. Pediatric. Priority 1. ETA 12 minutes by air." I will admit that I only heard this type of announcement a handful of times in four years, yet it was enough to make my heart skip a beat. It is the heralding of a collision between chaos and control, between good and evil, between fate and fortune.

Robert Scaer, a board-certified neurologist with over forty years of experience, defines a *trauma* as "a stressful event outside" our normal experiences that may cause physical or psychological damage.[84] According to Scaer, then, a *trauma* is an event that is typically physical in nature that is exerted upon us in such a way that harm is brought to us. This harm may be physical or psychological, or it may be both. Yet, how does this definition differ from that of a *crisis*? To answer this question, let us turn back to a couple of definitions that we looked

---

[84] Robert C. Scaer, *The Trauma Spectrum: Hidden Wounds and Human Resiliency* (New York: W. W. Norton and Co., 2005), 3.

at earlier. Many of my students have mentioned that they like the definition from Carkhuff and Berenson: "Crisis is a crisis because the individual knows no response to deal with a situation."[85] While this is a good definition, I prefer Richard James' definition, where he says that a "crisis is a perception or experiencing of an event or situation as an intolerable difficulty that exceeds the person's current resources and coping mechanisms."[86] As I mentioned earlier, the reason why I like this definition is because it resonates best with my experience in ministry— someone finds himself or herself in the middle of a situation that is so overwhelming that he or she feel helpless to react to the situation.

Yet, is there really a difference between *trauma* and *crisis*? I believe that there is and that it is not merely a matter of semantics. I understand a *trauma* as an event in which physical or psychological damage occurs to someone (ex., a car accident, a prolonged fall, being shot). To add to this, I understand a *crisis* as the *response* to the trauma that we have experienced (ex., depression, suicide, intense sorrow or suffering, death). Thus, the person who experiences the trauma can also experience some sort of crisis, although his or her family will only experience the crisis. In short, a *trauma* is an event that happens to us, while a *crisis* is our response to the event.

Now, I know that some of you are thinking to yourselves that crisis is not so static. In this, you are correct. What actually happens in the midst of a trauma is that a chain-reaction of events and responses are set off, with the eventual outcome remaining a mystery because the chain-reaction may take years to fully process. For example, a man in his late forties is brought to the Emergency Department after being involved in an ATV accident. Aside from sustaining a broken left leg, fractured pelvis, and broken left arm, he has several internal injuries— including internal bleeding. The patient is taken immediately to the operating room in order to stop the internal bleeding and assess the external and internal issues. The patient's outlook is quite grim, and the attending physician openly informs the family of this. The patient is intubated and on numerous medications to sustain his blood pressure and vital systems. Following numerous surgeries, the patient codes and

---

[85] Robert R. Carkhuff and Bernard G. Berenson, *Beyond Counseling and Therapy*, 2nd ed. (New York: Holt, Rinehart and Winston, 1977), 165.

[86] Richard K. James, *Crisis Intervention Strategies*, 6th ed. (Belmont, CA: Thomson/ Brooks-Cole, 2008), 3.

the medical team performs CPR on the patient for several minutes until a pulse is detected and the patient is stabilized. A few days later, the patient codes again, and while the medical team is able to stabilize the patient, it appears that the patient's systems are beginning to shut down. It is determined that the patient has now suffered a stroke. The attending physician suspects that the patient has suffered brain damage from the stroke, and he requests a brain-flow study to be conducted. The findings of the flow study are quite telling—the blood flow to the brain is beginning to cease, which means that the brain is beginning to swell. Eventually, the brain will swell to such a size that it will restrict the cerebral cortex from receiving blood and the patient will die. In fact, this is exactly what happens a few days later, with his family by his side.

The patient experiences the trauma of the accident, and while it is unclear of how much he suffered following, it is likely that he experienced the crisis of meeting death. What is clear is that his family does experience the crisis of seeing their loved one in this condition. Remember what I said earlier, while a patient can experience both the trauma and the ensuing crisis, the family can only experience the crisis that accompanies such a situation. Kenneth Mottram says that two things occur to those who are experiencing the situation from the other side of the bed.[87] First, their belief systems are challenged. As long as things run smoothly, we operate under the notion that we are in control of our lives. However, when we are confronted with such situations, our assumptions are tossed into the air. Most importantly, we are confronted with two perplexing questions: "Why did God allow this to happen?" and "Would God allow this to happen to me?" Of course, to ask these questions reflects a serious misunderstanding of the providence of God, yet they are questions that most people will ask in these situations. And it is important to remember that these situations are not appropriate for ratifying people's theology. Second, there is the experience of seeing the lifeless body of their loved one. Regardless of their age (I have learned that children remember things much earlier than is commonly accepted), everyone present will remember this scene. It is as if Fate stamps the scene in our minds, searing our souls with this moment of death.

Now what happens after the family leaves? Although most people

---

[87] Kenneth P. Mottram, *Caring for Those in Crisis: Facing Ethical Dilemmas with Patients and Families* (Grand Rapids, MI: Brazos Press, 2007), 40-41.

are overcome with grief, they find ways to cope with and process the loss. Some, however, succumb to the crisis, allowing themselves to be overcome with grief. Some may attempt suicide while others may suffer a psychotic break and drive their car off the road. Either of these situations are traumatic and will create a new series of crises that family members will suffer from. And just as with the initial crisis, some will process it appropriately and some will not. What is most important is that we are available to those who are suffering in critical moments so that the love of God may be offered to them.

## MINISTERING IN TRAUMATIC SITUATIONS

Kenneth Mottram writes, "One needs to be sensitive to the fact that they will remember every detail of the experience and that many of the details will be traumatic to them."[88] When we enter into traumatic situations as the representatives of God, we are truly entering into "the valley of the shadow of death" (Psalm 23:4). Everything will be heightened because those who are emotionally involved with the situation are experiencing an increase in adrenaline. This manifests itself in expressed anxiety— pacing, crying, shaking, loss of motor control, irritability, and anger. Here are some things to remember when entering into a traumatic crisis:

- *Be differentiated.* In a version of Friedman's idea, we are to share in the pain of the crisis without adding to it or taking away from it.
- *Remember that ministry is about being and not doing.* It is never more important than in times of crisis to remember than being present is enough.
- *Remember that we are there for the patient and/or the family.* We put our agendas aside and act in response to them. Our presence will always be appreciated, even by those with whom we are in discord with.
- *Respect the emotional time of the moment.* Our comfort is secondary to what they are feeling, even if what they are feeling is exaggerated.

---

[88] Ibid., 41.

The most important thing to remember is that we, as minister, are the presence of God in times in crisis! By nature of our pastoral identity and authority, we continue the ministry of the Incarnation by walking with them through this journey.

> How blessed is the man whose strength is in You, in whose heart are the highways to Zion! Passing through the valley of Baca they make it a spring. The early rain also covers it with blessings. They go from strength to strength, every one of them appears before God in Zion (Psalm 84:5-7).

Before we can get involved, we need to perform what I call a "spiritual triage." First, *find out exactly what is going on.* When we arrive at the hospital, we are going to be confronted with a great deal of chaos. It will be difficult to get any answers quickly, unless there is a chaplain or patient advocate readily available. Depending on the situation, there may be a great deal of misinformation that is being passed around. Thus, it will be important to discover the circumstances of the accident. As best as we can, it is important to also discover the condition of the patient. This is where being differentiated will come into play because hospital employees are more likely to pass along information to those who are level-headed. However, it is important to remember that simply because we are from the patient's church or are the patient's minister does not entitle us to any information outside of what has been shared with the family. It is also important to discover who is present and how they are related to the patient (especially if the patient is unfamiliar to you).

Second, *assess the condition of the family.* Some will be calm, some will be hysterical, some will be emotionally detached, and some will be in shock. It is important not to confuse being calm for being emotionally detached. Those who are emotionally detached often have a glazed look on their faces, while those who are calm are, well, quite level-headed. For some, being hysterical is how they deal with any situation that is left of center. And while we are more comfortable with people who are calm, it is impossible to make someone who is hysterical clam down by force. The best thing is honestly to let them get it out of their system because forcing them to calm down will only accentuate their histrionics. Third, *discover what spiritual resources are available.* Is there a chaplain available? Are they open to prayer? What are they expecting in terms of spiritual intervention? Once we have added to our own personal supply of resources, we are ready to get to work.

In terms of providing ministry in times of trauma and crisis, I can really only give five suggestions. Ministry in this area is an exercise in controlling (or more appropriately going along with) chaos. The more flexible we are, the more apt we will be to providing appropriate and effective crisis ministry. However, here are my guidelines:

1. *Relieve the chaplain, if you are comfortable being in the situation alone.* She or he will be of more service acting as a liaison between you and the medical staff, or there may be other situations in the facility that need their attention.
2. *Offer prayer that is realistic to the situation.* We offer prayer in the hope that God will work His wonders, yet there are times when praying for peace is fitting.
3. *Assist the family with the mundane (e.g., finding tissues, making calls, filling out paperwork).* These are actions that will speak louder than any pious words that we may offer.
4. *In death, help family with arrangements, but do not preach the funeral yet!* Family members are in shock at this point and will hear little of what is said. Thus, "taking care of business" is the only thing that needs to be done. Our chance to say what needs to be said will come in a few days.
5. *Remember, simply being there is often enough.* They may not remember what we said or did, yet they will remember that we were there. We are the staff that God uses to lead His people through the Valley.

In addition, I would add this suggestion from Mottram concerning seeing the patient who has been involved in an accident or who has died suddenly:

> If, as an advocate, you suspect possible injuries to the patient that might be traumatic for the family, I recommend you view the body before the family does to

help give your first impressions to the family as a means of minimizing the possible shock to them.[89]

In these critical moments, we are a shepherd, guiding frightened sheep along the path laid before them.

## POST-TRAUMATIC STRESS DISORDER

I wanted to include some material on Post-Traumatic Stress Disorder (PTSD) for two reasons. First, it is a greatly misunderstood condition. And, second, it does affect people who experience crises such as those we are currently discussing. The best source for learning more about PTSD is the National Institute for Mental Health. There has been a great deal written on the subject beyond the original concept of PTSD affecting only soldiers.[90] There has also been some excellent material written on the occurrence of PTSD in children and adolescents.[91] My intention here is not to exhaust the resources and offer you the "end-all and be-all" on PTSD; my intention is simply to introduce you, through Richard James' material, to the "symptoms" of PTSD, some behaviors that those affected with PTSD will display, and some approaches to counseling those who have PTSD. Before I go any further, however, let me make one thing perfectly clear: people who experience crises such as the ones we are discussing may exhibit PTSD-like symptoms. With some effort, you will be able to appropriately and effectively minister to them. However,

---

[89] Mottram, *Caring for Those in Crisis: Facing Ethical Dilemmas with Patients and Families*, 41.

[90] See Edna B. Foa, Terence E. Keane, Matthew J. Friedman, and Judith A. Cohen, ed., *Effective Treatments for PTSD: Practice Guidelines from the International Society for Traumatic Stress Studies*, 2nd ed. (New York: The Guilford Press, 2008); Deanna Rosenbloom and Mary Beth Williams, *Life After Trauma: A Workbook for Healing*, 2nd ed. (New York: The Guilford Press, 2010); and Glenn Schiraldi, *The Post-Traumatic Stress Disorder Sourcebook: A Guide to Healing, Recovery, and Growth*, 2nd ed. (New York: McGraw-Hill, 2009).

[91] See Kimberly Cheryl, *Shattered Reality: A Mother's Story* (Seattle: CreateSpace, 2008); Judith A. Cohen, Anthony P. Mannarino, and Esther Deblinger, *Treating Trauma and Traumatic Grief in Children and Adolescents* (New York: The Guilford Press, 2006); and Eliana Gil, *Helping Abused and Traumatized Children: Integrating Directive and Nondirective Approaches* (New York: The Guilford Press, 2006). As a side note, anything by Eliana Gil would be helpful when working with children in a counseling context, especially her work on play therapy.

you should consider referring someone with full-blown PTSD (such as a war veteran or an abuse survivor) to a professional therapist. There is no shame in referring someone who suffers from this tragic condition if you do not feel adequate to the task.

How do we "diagnose" whether or not someone has PTSD? James is most instructive in this manner, as he provides the following symptoms: first, the person has been exposed to a traumatic event in which the threat of death or serious injury was presented to him/her. James also notes that part of the assessment process should include an *"attempt to determine if there has been exposure to prior trauma*, particularly when the crisis seems to have occurred spontaneously, with no clear, immediate, precipitating stimulus."[92] Second, the person will continue reliving the experience in at least one of the following ways:

- Recurrent and intrusive distressing recollections of the event;
- Recurrent nightmares of the event;
- Flashback episodes, hallucinations, or disassociation from reality;
- Intense psychological distress on exposure to internal and external cues that symbolize or resemble an aspect of the crisis;
- Physiologic reactivity on exposure to events that symbolize or resemble some aspect of the trauma.

Third, the person will persistently avoid stimulation in at least three of the following ways:

- Attempts to avoid thoughts, discussions, or feelings associated with the event;
- Attempts to avoid activities, people, or situations that stimulate recollections of the event;
- Unable to recall particular and significant aspects of the event;
- Diminished interest in significant activities;
- Feels emotionally detached from others;
- Affected by numbing sensations that restrict activity;
- Has a sense of a foreshortened future.

---

[92] James, *Crisis Intervention Strategies*, 129.

Fourth, the person suffers from an increase in the arousal of their nervous system that can be attributed to at least two causes:

- Difficulty falling or staying asleep;
- Irritability or outbursts of anger;
- Difficulty concentrating on tasks;
- Hypervigilence or unexplained paranoia;
- Exaggerated reactions to nonthreatening stimuli.

Fifth, the person suffers "clinically significant distress or impairment in social, occupational, or other critical areas of life."[93] Examples of such areas include maintaining a job, allowing a marriage to end in divorce, or developing an addiction to narcotics and controlled substances. In children, this symptom is more difficult to assess, although some examples would include pulling away from cherished activities or allowing a positive, loving relationship with his or her parent(s) to dissolve. Finally, the person experiences a severe change in personality that has long-term effects.

Now, what are some behaviors that are exhibited by those who are suffering from PTSD? James says that there are five primary forms of "maladaptive behaviors":

- *Death Imprint*—The experience confronts the person with his/her mortality where only a sense of invulnerability reigned before. Instead of developing a healthy awareness of death, however, the person begins dwelling on death.
- *Survivor's Guilt*—Those who survive traumatic experiences feel guilty for surviving when others involved do not. They routinely blame themselves for the event, and will even seek to terminate their own lives because they feel it should have been them who died instead of the other(s).
- *Desensitization*—On the other end of the spectrum, the person experiences a vacuum of emotion. If they do experience emotions, they are what we typically refer to as negative emotions such as hate, rage, or envy. However, it is important to remember that

---

[93] Ibid., 128.

emotions are not good or bad; it is what we do with them that determine their intrinsic value.

- *Estrangement*—The person begins to pull away from significant relationships, feeling that every encounter is another trauma waiting to happen. The person will also likely develop a "victim mentality" as he or she becomes more and more isolated from those willing to offer assistance.

- *Emotional Enmeshment*—On the other end of the relationship spectrum, the person may become so emotionally involved that they are unable to control their emotions. On one hand, they volunteer all kinds of time to be involved with their children. On the other hand, they beat their kids for no reason whatsoever. This develops a dysfunctional system of control that, unless treated, will have disastrous outcomes. [94]

Finally, is there any chance of recovery for those who suffer from PTSD? Fortunately, the answer is that there is, thanks in large part to the massive work done by civilian and military medical and mental health professionals. Brende and Parson, in their work of combining the theories and approaches of some of the leading theorists and practitioners in the field of PTSD, have developed the following five-step approach to treating those with PTSD:

1. *Emergency or outcry stage*—This stage is equivalent with the "fight or flight" reaction that comes with the combination of adrenaline and crisis. This stage will last as long as the person allows it to, and a great sense of relief will come when the person allows the stage to end.

2. *Emotional numbing and denial stage*—The person protects her or his emotional well-being by enveloping themselves in an emotional cocoon. In doing so, the person is able to reduce anxiety and cope with the situation. However, some never come out of the cocoon.

3. *Intrusive-repetitive stage*—The person begins having numerous troubling experiences such as nightmares, hallucinations, and

---

[94] Ibid., 138-139.

violent mood swings. The person either seeks out assistance on his or her own, or is required to seek help.

4. *Reflective-transition stage*—The person accepts that the situation was beyond their control, begins to constructively and effectively process the trauma, and seeks to develop a healthy outlook on life.

5. *Integration stage*—As with any form of grief, the person successfully integrates this experience into his or her life and becomes a source of healing and energy for a healthy future. [95]

As nice as this sounds, it is highly unlikely that someone who is suffering from PTSD will move through the stages this neatly. Typically, victims of PTSD will cycle through a series of lower-level and overlapping emotional, physical, and spiritual crises before he or she is finally able to begin the recovery process.

[95] Joel Osler Brende and Erwin Randolph Parson, *Vietnam Veterans: The Road to Recovery* (New York: Plenum Publishing Co., 1985), 185-186; cited in James, *Crisis Intervention Strategies*, 142.

# CHAPTER 11
# DEATH OF AN ADULT

In all its grandeur, death is about endings. And few have offered more insightful thoughts than those provided by Paul Tillich (1886-1965):

> It is our destiny and the destiny of everything in our world that we must come to an end. Every end that we experience in nature and mankind says to us in a loud voice, "You also will come to an end!" It may reveal itself in the farewell to a place where we have loved for a long time, the separation from the fellowship of intimate associates, the death of someone near to us. Or it may become apparent to us in the breakdown of a work which gave meaning to us, the ending of a whole period of life, the approach of old age, or even in the melancholy side of nature visible in the autumn. All this tells us, "You also will come to an end."[96]

However, the inescapable nature of death is not the only aspect of humanity that I wish for us to reflect on. While it is true that none of us will complete the journey through this life without encountering death at least once, it is also true that every death affects more than just the one who dies. A singular death affects an entire community. Whether it is the respected congregational elder who is deeply involved in his community or the homeless woman who lives off of the charity of others, their deaths are equal in their overall affect—the loss of each will radically alter the community in which they live:

---

[96] Paul Tillich, "The Eternal Now," in *The Meaning of Death*, ed. Herman Feifel (New York: McGraw-Hill, 1959), 30.

> The death of one person affects all with whom he or she has dealt. Death is an eminently social event. It breaks in on a community like an echoing, ricocheting sound reminding us all of our finitude. It rearranges relationships in families. Ministry amid death is best understood, not just individualistically as care for a single person, but also interpersonally for the family, friends, and wider community as well.

Without ruling out confrontation or challenge, ministry to the dying is usually one of quiet consolation, palliation, and hope, seeking to comfort those who mourn (Matt. 5:4), "to build up the brokenhearted. . .to give them garlands instead of ashes, oil of gladness instead of mourner's tears, a garment of splendor for the heavy heart" (Isa. 61:1, 3).[97]

Death has a powerful affect on us. It shapes our understanding of God's providence and our finitude. And it is, without a doubt, the one thing that all will experience in one way or another. Thus, we will look at how to minister to the dying, how to minister in time of death, how to minister in time of bereavement, and how to minister in the post-funeral time.

## MINISTRY TO THE DYING

Douglas Purnell writes, "Hospitals are places where sharp existential questions are shaped. . . .It is in hospitals that most people are born, suffer, and die, so it is no surprise that deep existential questions are often shaped in hospitals."[98] Simply being admitted to the hospital causes people to take stock of their lives and reflect on things that they would otherwise not do so. And from my experience, dying patients are even more aware of the brevity of life and the seriousness of preparing to pass between this life and the next. In no other situation than in this one is it important to simply be present:

---

[97] Thomas C. Oden, *Pastoral Theology: Essentials for Ministry* (New York: HarperCollins, 1983), 296-297.

[98] Douglas Purnell, *Conversation as Ministry: Stories and Strategies for Confident Caregiving* (Cleveland, OH: Pilgrim Press, 2003), 139.

> A minister entered a hospital room one day where the patient was terminally ill. She knew that she was dying. She already had a visitor. The patient was crying and the visitor was saying, "Now, now. Don't cry. Everything's going to be all right. God is going to make everything all right." With that the visitor left. The minister pulled a chair up beside the bed, took the patient's hand and sat there in silence. He said nothing. After about ten minutes, the patient said, "You're such a comfort to me." He had not said one word![99]

People who are dying do not need to be shielded from the reality the situation nor do they need to be reminded of it at every moment. People who are experiencing life slip from their bodies are acutely aware of their situation. I once visited a man who was on the Oncology unit. The visit was to complete a consult from our Palliative Care team. The man had decided that at the stage of his illness—he was in fourth-stage liver failure—that he was done with medical treatment and simply wanted to go home to die. As I spoke with him, he told me that he was not afraid of dying nor did he have any plans to end his life prematurely. He simply wanted to meet his end in the comfortable surroundings of his small apartment rather than in the sterile confines of the hospital room. As with most people who have accepted their condition, he was not looking for counsel. He was looking for someone to listen to him and speak a prayer on his behalf. By the very nature of his physical condition as opposed to mine, he was far more experienced in the realm of dying. Before we go any further, reflect on these words from Thomas Oden:

> If dying is something that one can fully do right only once, then we can draw this ironic conclusion: being alive, and therefore having as yet missed the experience of death, is, oddly enough, an intrinsic presupposition of ministry. So the minister, in not having died, is on equal footing with members of the dying person's family but not with the dying person, who knows existentially more

---

[99] Robert C. Shannon and J. Michael Shannon, *Practical Ministry in the Real World* (Joplin, MO: College Press Publishing Co., 1997), 90.

than the minister does about the experience. This is an odd point, but I am determined to make it: ministry does well to acknowledge its critical lack of experience and to listen carefully to the unparalleled experience of those who are dying.[100]

This being said, it is important to remember that we do not come alongside the patient as an expert, one who knows assuredly what lies ahead, but as a guide who has walked the path partway before. As Morpheus in *The Matrix*, we can show them the door, but only they can walk through it. Thus, Oden provides us with the following guidelines in providing care and counseling to the dying:[101]

- *God does not test us beyond our strength.* Even in death, God is with us. As Paul reminds us, "No temptation has overtaken you but such as is common to man; and God is faithful, who will not allow you to be tempted beyond what you are able, but with the temptation will provide the way of escape also, so that you will be able to endure it" (1 Corinthians 10:13). Death is part of life, thus facing death is not beyond our strength through God.
- *Jesus himself is the best pattern for the Christian's meeting with death.* As one elderly man taught me early on in my clinical training, nothing gives the person of faith more strength in the face of death than prayer. No tricks, no specials, no gimmicks. When we are confronted with the "ultimate horizon," there is little else we should do than pray. That's what Jesus did (Mark 9:2-8, 14:32-42), thus we should no less.
- *The pastoral duty to assist persons in their meeting with death may require diverse interpersonal competencies.* Death affects everyone differently. As Shannon and Shannon remind us, dying patients will want to talk about the elephant in the room. Yet some of the family will not. They will want to ignore it, deny it, or refuse to allow the dying to talk about it. "Your job is to listen. That's hard to do. . . .Your only responsibility to be available. You are not responsible for succeeding in leading them to face death

[100] Oden, *Pastoral Theology: Essentials for Ministry*, 301-302.
[101] Ibid., 302-303.

calmly. Most of them will do that, but your only responsibility is to be there, to listen, and to care."[102]

- *Anyone who is aware that choice implies negation knows that freedom is no unmixed blessing.* Choosing to sign a DNR form means that a patient will meet death in a certain way, just as placing a patient on a ventilator and putting them on "Full Code" status means that he or she will meet death in a certain way. Every choice we make in how we meet our end means that we make another choice in how we do not meet it. Our job as ministers is not to argue or challenge those decisions. Our job is to respect them and honor them.

Thus, we seek to assist the dying patient in the creation of a context for understanding their terminal condition. Purnell offers us this two-step approach to creating this context: "There are, I think, at least two stages in talking with people about dying. The first is a look back at life in which people seek to integrate their life experiences. The second is to look forward to, to anticipate, to enter the moment that is death."[103]

In order to create this context, Switzer suggests several needs that dying patients that must be addressed:

- Dying patients need to be allowed to express their feelings.
- Dying patients need to be surrounded with loved ones.
- Dying patients need to know that their lives have been meaningful.
- Dying patients need to discover meaning in their moment of suffering.
- Dying patients need to feel useful.
- Dying patients need to exert some control over their lives.
- Dying patients need to receive consistent messages.
- Dying patients need to be reminded of God's presence in their lives.
- Dying patients need to be encouraged to let go of life and embrace death.[104]

---

[102] Shannon and Shannon, *Practical Ministry in the Real World*, 90-91.

[103] Purnell, *Conversation as Ministry: Stories and Strategies for Confident Caregiving*, 140-141.

[104] David K. Switzer, *Pastoral Care Emergencies*, Creative Pastoral Care and Counseling Series (Minneapolis: Fortress Press, 2000), 85-92.

Helping meet these needs will carry dying patients and their families a great distance as they cross the Valley of the Shadow of Death.

## MINISTRY IN TIME OF DEATH

There was a series on the Spike channel called "1000 Ways to Die." This series showcased ways that people have died, ranging from the unexplained to the utterly bizarre. However, I have come to conclusion that there are really only four ways people die—comfortably medicated, uncontrolled anguish, instantly in a tragic accident, or hooked up to a ventilator. I have been with families when a patient has died in each of these situations, and none is any easier than the other. I have seen family members literally try to take the deceased home with them because they're "just asleep" and I have seen family members calmly walk away from a patient who died in a tragic accident. What is important to remember is that every person will respond to the death in their own fashion.

Most of what we discussed in our last chapter on trauma will be useful when called to the death. However, there are some particulars that we must be aware of, especially when we are called to minister in an acute situation. For the most part, there are really only four things that we can do when we are ministering in the time of death: pray, pass out tissues, tell family members "I'm sorry," and offer hugs. Saying anything pious or pithy would simply be a waste of our breath. The thing that we want to people to remember is that we were there for them. Yet, when you are called to the Emergency Department for a death as a result of a traumatic accident or cardiac arrest, it is important to remember the following:

- The family will be in shock for most of the time. They will not actually begin to grieve until they see the body of their loved one at the funeral.
- Just because you are the minister does not mean that you get any special treatment. The medical staff has a job to do, and they will allow you to view the body with the family when *they* are ready to do so.
- If the patient had to be intubated, the tube will still be in place when you view the body until the Medical Examiner releases

the body to the funeral home or takes custody of the body for an autopsy. For example, it is state law in West Virginia that the Medical Examiner be contacted when a patient dies within twenty-fours of admission even if the attending physician is 100% sure of what killed the patient. I would imagine that this is fairly standard.

- Also, although they will try their hardest to make the body presentable, you must be prepared for the worst physically.

- Eventually, the family will need to provide the medical staff with a funeral home to contact for picking up the body. If the family is unsure of who to use, you may provide them counsel about options.

- This is not the time to begin making arrangements regarding the funeral or who will provide food for the mourning family. Those things should be taken care of in the following day or two. What is important at this time is to provide the family the space to experience the shock of death.

Most of this will also serve us well when we respond to deaths in the ICU or on a general medical floor. It has always been my custom to walk the family out of the hospital, both as a located minister and as a chaplain. If you are the minister or pastoral caregiver, make sure that everyone has rides home and that you or another minister has touched base with the immediate family regarding meeting with the funeral director to make arrangements.

## MINISTRY IN TIME OF BEREAVEMENT

This section is not going to focus on the funeral itself as much as on preparing for the funeral. Most "minister's manuals" will provide outlines for standard funeral services. Although I promote a tailored approach to funeral services, these can be helpful when you are just beginning in ministry, new to a congregation, or required by your local leadership functionary to do so. What I want to discuss here is how to guide the family through the tactical steps of the bereavement period. Naturally, there will be a lot of paperwork that the family will need to tend to. If the patient was on Medicare, had life insurance, received veteran's benefits, or was entitled to any other form of benefit, each of those organizations will need to be contacted. The family may not necessarily know how to begin this phase. Being able to be a calm and steady guide through this tedious phase will be of great blessing to them.

Also, there is the part about the funeral. Now, it is important to remember that the funeral business is a service industry like everything else. Funeral directions, while they provide a valuable service, are also looking to make a profit off of that service. Some funeral directors are honest and forthright and will work with families to create a respectful burial program. Some, however, will only try to milk the family for all they can. This is when knowing the funeral director comes in handy. I will share a little piece of advice that was passed on to me by my college ministry professor—talk with the funeral directors early in your arrival and keep copies of their price lists available. Ask to meet with the family before they go to the funeral director, or offer to meet them at the funeral home. Practice your attentive listening as the funeral director and family talk about the arrangements, and be their advocate if need be.

When it comes to preparing for the funeral, I recommend asking the family to get together so that you can talk with them about the deceased. Ask them to share stories about their loved one so that you can get a good picture of his or her life. This is especially helpful if you are new to the congregation or if you were asked to perform the service for someone outside your congregation. As you preparing your eulogy and funeral sermon, be sure to include some of these stories. This lets the family know that you were paying attention and that you are allowing them to honor their loved one through their own words, even if they do not speak publicly. The funeral is a time to honor the deceased. Yet it is also a time to provide comfort and solace to the family. This is especially important during the graveside ceremony. This is the last time that the family will "see" their loved one until they cross over from this life to the next, and it is important to provide a message of hope and peace to the mourning family.

## MINISTRY POST-FUNERAL

Although we have moved beyond the crisis by the time the funeral service ends, it is vital that we not gloss over this important phase of the grief process. As we mentioned in our section on grief, the pain of losing a loved one is greatest at the initial loss. As Object Relational Theory teaches, the pain of the loss will diminish through time, although it will never completely dwindle away. We will always miss our loved ones, we will always grieve them, we will always need a shoulder to cry on, and we will always need to someone to pray for us. Here are some tips to remember when ministering to those who are grieving the loss of a loved one:

- There should be an immediate follow-up visit within a week of the funeral, and additional follow-up visits over the course of the next three months.
- The bereaved need to be allowed to express their emotions regarding the death in a healthy, productive, and safe way.
- The bereaved will need to be taught how to grow through their grief, processing their loss constructively so that their faith is enriched.
- The bereaved should either be connected with grief support groups, or the minister or trained pastoral caregiver should facilitate such a group.
- If necessary, the minister or pastoral caregiver should refer the bereaved on to a specialist in grief therapy if the bereaved is not working through their grief in a healthy manner.

As with ministry in the moment of crisis, sometimes simply being present and available will make the most difference as family members learn to live on without their loved ones.

## CHAPTER 12

# PASTORAL CARE OF CHILDREN

## PEDIATRIC PASTORAL CARE

When it comes to pastoral care, good practice is good practice. In terms of tactics and tools, much of what was discussed in our lesson on ministering to adults will be helpful when ministering to children and adolescents. While developmental concerns should be taken into account, pastoral care is not like youth ministry and education. It is a ministry of the moment, meaning our task is to respond to what is presented to us. Prayer, anointing, holding hands, reading scripture and listening are universal ministry methods (trust me). However, I would like to share some suggestions for visiting children and adolescents who may be hospitalized:

- Take note of the environment and the condition of the patient and his/her family.
- Ask him/her how she feels that day.
- Evaluate how well the child understands why he/she is in the hospital. Kids are more aware of what is going on than we give them credit for. Good doctors can explain the nature of the illness or injury in ways that children can understand. It will important to help them process this spiritually.
- Use concrete language. Abstract concepts escape younger children.
- Encourage children to express how they actually feel, not just placate adults.
- Explore what children are hiding in their "secret places" and encourage them to reveal that to their parents, guardians and caregivers.

- Check out support systems.
- Gauge the child's (and the parents' or guardians') relationship with the medical team
- Offer to help.
- Assess the child's spatial orientation. Do they understand how long they have been hospitalized? Are they aware of what is going on outside their room?
- Commit to making return visits. I enjoy visiting kids because kids are genuine. They also appreciate someone who comes to see them just because they are there.

Here are a couple of other tips that I have learned in my years of chaplaincy. First, wear a smile when you enter the room. Kids can sense when you are faking your interest in being there. Second, show them your hands. This is especially important when you are visiting a child that does not know you. When you show them your hands, they trust that you will not poke, prod, or jab them in some way. This will build trust. Last, have something like stickers or bubbles that you can leave with the child. Do this for no other reason than to brighten the child's day.

## THEOLOGICAL REFLECTION ON CHILDREN AND DYING

To be sure, there are fewer topics that can stop a conversation than speaking about the death of a child. In many ways, it is more taboo than suicide (our next lesson). We are so overcome with weakness that we can barely utter the words that reveal our realization—when children die, we remember that we are merely mortals, that we are "a vapor that appears for a little while and then vanishes away" (James 4:14). Yet, throughout most of history, children were not accorded the position of reverence that they have been given in our day and time. There was once a time when children were lumped in with slaves, women, and property—their value was only based on what the father (or master) could get from them. However, today, children are the center of our universe, both positively and negatively. As a father myself, there is nothing that I would not to do protect my children, yet I must be stern with them when need be. Although, when my daughter bats her eyes or my son cracks his smile, I often release my grip on discipline—something my wife and I term as being a "caver."

Although the Bible is remarkably near-silent in terms of suicide, it speaks often about the death of children. In many ways, we can draw modern applications to these ancient stories. One of the first stories that we might think of is the story of Abraham and Isaac. After decades of asking God for a son, Abraham and Sarah are finally blessed with a child. Then one day God comes to Abraham and asks him to sacrifice his young offspring (Genesis 22:1-2). I can only imagine Abraham's anxiety as he made the march up that distant hill, knowing that he would come down alone after worshipping God. I can remember Hailey's mom and dad, sitting around her bed, as she slowly and painfully died from medulloblastoma, a type of pediatric brain cancer. They knew that this could be the last time that they ever bring her to the hospital. As the hours drug on, they held out hope that God would deliver a miracle. Only this time there would be no ram caught in the thicket. Hailey died with her family around her bed, quietly and peacefully and with permission to do so.

We may also think of the cataclysmic tragedy of the final plague brought upon Egypt because of one man's pride. We often think that the plague only struck the firstborn son of each household. However, as the animated *The Prince of Egypt* (1998) reminds us, the plague was destined to strike every firstborn: "and all the firstborn in the land of Egypt shall die, from the firstborn of the Pharaoh who sits on his throne, even to the firstborn of the slave girl who is behind the millstones; all the firstborn of the cattle as well" (Exodus 11:5). If my family had been Egyptian, my father, my son, my father-in-law, my brother-in-law, and I would have all perished.

Today, drug addiction has unleashed a new plague upon the firstborn; only this plague is no respecter of gender. We can also think of the death of Absalom (2 Samuel 18). His death reminds me of a *Sports Illustrated* article about teenagers killing other teenagers over Nikes that I read when I was younger. The characters and the context were different, yet the outcome was still the same—greed causes great calamity upon those who seek refuge in her web. David lost not only one son, but two. Following his adulterous and murderous liaison with Bathsheba, God "struck the child that Uriah's widow bore to David, so that he was very sick" (2 Samuel 12:15). Although David prayed and fasted, the child eventually died. There have been numerous times when I have been called to the Neonatal ICU to pray over or baptize an infant that has died.

Finally, we may call to mind the story of Jesus and the Syrophonecian woman who comes to him begging for her daughter to be healed (Mark 7:24-30). This mother, whose daughter was possessed by an evil spirit, came to Jesus for healing. Yet, she found an unwilling Physician, much like many parents do today when they bring their children to emergency rooms and walk-in clinics. However, she was determined to find a cure for her daughter, and showed herself to be strong in spirit and wise in mind by participating in Jesus' bantering. Impressed by her faith, Jesus healed the little girl.

To be sure, there is little that instills more fear and anxiety into the hearts of ministers and pastoral caregivers more than be called to the hospital because of a sick child. As a chaplain, my practice was typically to leave the family in the hands of the minister when he or she arrives. However, I can remember one particular instance where abuse led to the death of an infant, and the minister asked me to stay. As John Hesch writes,

> Ministers who otherwise feel confident in their roles and their ability to help may feel inadequate when faced with the situation of a dying child. This is understandable since the death of a child is certainly one of life's greatest human tragedies. Precisely because of the severely traumatic nature of such an event, the minister's presence and help may be extremely important.[105]

Much of what we have discussed in terms of the practical side of ministering in times of death can also be applied to the death of children. However, there is a mystery that surrounds how to minister to children who are terminally ill and how to minister to grieving families. Although I cannot promise to lift the fog entirely, my goal in this lesson is to at least provide you with a lamp that you may use to give light in dark times. We will begin by looking at the reality that children know when they are dying and how to appropriately minister to them, then we will look at the place of honesty in such situations, and then conclude by discussing how to minister to grieving families.

---

[105] John B. Hesch, *Clinical Pastoral Care for Hospitalized Children and Their Families* (New York/Mahwah, NJ: Paulist Press, 1987), 145.

## MINISTERING TO TERMINALLY-ILL CHILDREN

When we use the term "terminally ill," we are actually using a misnomer. In truth, we are all "terminal," in that we all have an appointment with death. It is also a misnomer in that the term is only used in reference to those who are suffering from a form of cancer. However, from a medical perspective, the phrase "terminally ill" can also be applied to those who have suffered a severe injury and have no chance of recovery. In such times, a sense of openness and reverence is needed. Children who are nearing the end of their earthly journey need the sacred space to express themselves.

In research she conducted for her doctorate in nursing practice, Eugenia Waechter argued that elementary-aged children who are suffering from a terminal illness do experience and express apprehension about their impending deaths. Waechter believed that shielding children from the reality of their situation only prevented ill children from meeting their deaths in a mature fashion.[106] She talked with several children and found that terminally ill children struggle with the following feelings, whether adults admit it or not.[107] First, there is the feeling of *helplessness*. Children often feel helpless, given their lesser ability when placed against the adult world. Yet this feeling is greater when poked and prodded by nurses, respiratory therapists, doctors, phlebotomists, and X-ray technicians. Second, there is the feeling of *distress*. When Waechter conducted her research the pediatric nursing profession was still in its infancy. Children's hospitals and units specifically geared to treating children were rare. As a result, children admitted to experiencing a lack of support, helpfulness, and encouragement from their caretakers. It is my perception that this feeling is still prevalent as, even at a hospital that has dedicated pediatric units, there are emergency department nurses that openly refuse to treat pediatric patients. Third, there is the feeling of *loneliness*. Although pediatric units often have extended visiting hours, parents and other family members are not always able to be by their child's side. Thus, the attentive minister can be a welcome friend in times between visits. Finally, there is the feeling of *anger*. In our civil society, we

---

[106] Eugenia H. Waechter, "Children's Awareness of Fatal Illness," *American Journal of Nursing* 71 (June 1971): 1168.

[107] Ibid., 1170-1172.

are encouraged to repress our anger. Even when we have the right to be angry, we are told not to be so. It is even more so with children. However, children have just as much right to be angry about dying as any adult. Children need to be allowed to express themselves so that they may meet their death as maturely as possible, even if that means allowing them a catharsis as screaming or weeping.

I remember the last time I talked with Amber. Her parents asked me to talk with her in private due to the numerous times that I had visited with them. Our conversations had been mostly menial, but always pleasant and prayer-focused. I knew that our conversations would end soon. It was something that she, too, knew. I simply asked her how she was feeling. At first, she was hesitant, believing that children should not express themselves. However, I could tell that she needed to say what was on her heart. After sitting in silence and letting my question hang between us, she finally said, "I am so (expletive) angry!" She then apologized for cursing. She explained that she was angry about dying, about missing senior prom, angry about not going to college, angry about not getting married, and angry about not having children of her own. After talking for nearly an hour about how she felt, she simply asked me to pray that God would give her the courage to face her death. She knew that God was waiting to receive her with open arms, that God would heal her and restore her as she waited for her parents to join her. I was not on-call when Amber died a few nights later. The chaplain who was present relayed a message from her parents. They wanted to thank me for my ministry to Amber and to them. According to her mother, one of her last audible statements was, "I'm ready to die and be with God."

## THE VALUE OF HONESTY

When ministering to children, it is often assumed that being quiet about their condition—or the condition of their siblings—is the best approach. We believe that it is better to shield them from the gruesomeness of illness so that they may retain their purity and innocence. We hope to instill within them a rose-colored picture of how the world works. Yet, all it takes is one single encounter in order to reshape reality. Just think of the first time you saw someone seriously injured or saw someone you knew die. How did that alter your perception of reality? Children, in order to live life appropriately, need for us to be honest about matters of life and death. As James writes, "Some people believe that children should be shielded and protected from exposure to death and loss. The research suggests, however, that bereaved children will make healthier adjustments to loss if they are informed about the loss truthfully and actively."[108] In addition, Hesch indicates that children who are presented with a "false cheerfulness" about death will "become even more anxious about death and may feel isolated from others or even rejected by them."[109] Thus, it is vitally important that we be open and clear about illness and death with both the children who are patients and their siblings. This exposure should be slow and controlled, allowing for the child's individual development process.

My children, who are 10 and 9, are aware that death is part of life. Their current belief structure is that when they die, they will go to Heaven and be with God. My son is okay with this, yet my daughter is not because she does not want to leave her friends. Reminding her that being with God is much better offers no assurance because that is beyond her reasoning ability. They knew that I spent my nights praying and talking to sick people. They also knew that, occasionally, some of my patients do not leave the hospital alive. This, I believe, is a healthy approach because I think it has prepared my children to greet death in a healthy way.

## MINISTERING TO GRIEVING FAMILIES

Ministering to grieving families is much more in-depth than ministering to families when an adult dies. It is difficult to explain why it is different, yet it is. There is something different in the context of grief when a child is involved. And when it comes to ministering in times of grief and grief counseling, there are few who are better than William Worden. Worden, who teaches at the Harvard University Medical School and has a psychological practice in California, has been writing and lecturing on grief therapy for over forty years. He has conducted research with Elisabeth Kubler-Ross and his textbook is considered the standard in the field of grief therapy.

It may seem unfair to classify the typical approaches of parents

---

[108] Richard K. James, *Crisis Intervention Strategies*, 6th ed. (Belmont, CA: Thomson Higher Education/Brooks-Cole, 2008), 369.
[109] Hesch, *Clinical Pastoral Care of Hospitalized Children and Their Families*, 152.

to grieving as unhealthy, yet they are. As Worden explains, parents who lose a child usually approach the grieving process in one of three ways.[110] First, parents will attempt to replace the lost child by bearing another one. Some couples will find sexual attraction rekindled and will attempt to fill the void by replacing their lost child with a new one. The reason why this is unhealthy is because it disrespects the child who has died and it places an unfair burden on the newborn to live up to a set of expectations that should never be placed upon a child. Second, parents will attempt to erase the existence of the child they have lost. Clothes will be donated, furniture will be sold, photographs will be tossed, and memories will be blotted out. Third, parents will develop an obsession over the dead child. I remember one father who wanted to take the medical equipment home and set up his daughter's room exactly as it was in the hospital. I remember another mother who kept her son's room exactly as it was on the day he entered the hospital—pajamas on the floor, bed unmade, backpack next to his dresser, and a book on his desk. When I met her for a counseling session, it had been ten years since her son's death. It is important, when ministering to grieving parents, that parents be given time and space to grieve the loss of their child. When a child dies, the parents are not only mourning the loss of their little boy or little girl. They are also mourning the loss of part of their self. When they die, part of us dies as well.

It is also common for surviving parents and siblings to experience guilt. Worden, citing some research conducted by Miles and Demi, points out that there are five types of grief that are common among grieving parents and siblings.[111] First, there is *cultural guilt*. Here, parents suffer from the cultural expectation placed upon parents to protect their children. Second, there is *casual guilt*. Here, parents suffer from the guilt brought on from their negligence or involvement in the child's death. Some parents will also feel guilty is the child died from an inherited medical condition. Third, there is *moral guilt*. Here, parents suffer from a form of guilt brought on because they believe that they violated some type of moral or spiritual law. As in the story of David and Bathsheba mentioned above, they will feel that they are being punished for some

---

[110] J. William Worden, *Grief Counseling and Grief Therapy: A Handbook for the Mental Health Practitioner*, 4th ed. (New York: Springer Publishing Co., 2009), 222-224.
[111] Ibid., 225.

wrongdoing that has gone unforgiven. Fourth, there is *survival guilt*. Survival guilt, likely the most common form of guilt, occurs in parents who were involved in an accident with the child. The child dies and they survive, thus they are burdened with the unanswerable question of why did they survive and their child did not. Finally, there is *recovery guilt*. Here, parents feel guilty when they make the commitment to move on with their lives and to work through the grief cycle. They believe that they are dishonoring the memory of their child by moving on. Yet this is exactly what should happen.

One of Worden's greatest accomplishments to the field of grief therapy is the development of his "tasks of mourning." [112] By helping grieving parents through these "tasks" (and this paradigm can be used for anyone who is mourning), we can help them place their deceased child in the proper place in their memory and begin moving on with life. Here is the process: First, grieving parents must accept the reality of the loss. When people first hear the news of a death, they are in shock. This shock is actually a natural defense mechanism that gives us the necessary adrenaline to make it through the initial crisis. Some people will allow this state of shock to last for years because they cannot bear the burden of accepting the reality of the situation. However, until they do, those in grief cannot hope to heal from their loss. Second, grieving parents must process the pain caused by grief. Just like with forgiveness, we must be willing to process the hurt we feel. We can either allow the pain to fester and rot our souls, or we can turn this pain into healing energy that can provide us with purpose and peace. Some are able to process their pain through prayer, while others may need regular therapy. Whatever it is, encourage grieving family members to find a treatment for their pain. Third, grieving parents must adjust to life without the deceased. As much as we resist it, we adjust to change and growth all the time. Dealing with a death is just another form of change, only it is a painful change. However, it is a trickier change to navigate. In adjusting to life without our child, we must make external adjustments (reshaping our families to be smaller), internal adjustments (reshaping our dreams for our child and reshaping our sense of self as a parent), and spiritual adjustments (reshaping our sense of God and of our religious beliefs). Finally, grieving parents must "find an enduring connection with the deceased in the

---

[112] Ibid., 39-53.

midst of embarking on a new life."[113] In doing so, parents make the resolution to live a normal, productive life. Yes, they will still grieve; yet they resolve not to allow that grief to dominate their lives. Instead, they develop a sort of on-going relationship with their deceased child. It may come in the form of visiting the child's grave annually, baking a cake on their birthday, or creating some other form of special ceremony where the child is remembered.

However, parents are not the only ones who need care and concern when a child dies. Many times, siblings are left out of the equation when it comes to grieving children. Worden reminds us that children who lose siblings find this time confusing because they are unsure of what to tell their friends and they often feel guilty for being happy when around friends or other family members.[114] I remember being at the bedside of a long-term care patient who had become one of my favorites to visit with during my clinical training. I rarely saw his brother, primarily because he was always in school when his brother was in the hospital. On this particular visit, the brother, sensing that his brother was getting worse, stepped out of the room for a moment. I stepped out after him and asked him if he was okay. He asked me if it was okay for him to hope that his brother dies quickly and peacefully. He said that he wanted his parents to be happy again. He loved his brother very much, yet he also could tell how his brother's condition wore on his parents, especially his mother. This is why it is important to remember the siblings.[115] Children are often more aware of what is going on than we give them credit for, thus we should be just as ready to minister to them as we are their parents and their ailing siblings.

## CONCLUDING REMARKS

I wish that I could tell you that there was some magic spell that you could cast so that you would never have to minister in this type of situation. However, it will eventually happen. I never had to deal with the death of a child in seven years of congregational ministry. However, three weeks into my clinical training, I dealt with three in one twenty-four hour

[113] Ibid., 50.
[114] Ibid., 224.
[115] See Betty Davies, "After a Child Dies: Helping the Siblings," in *Hospice Care for Children*, 157-171.

period. I learned that there is really nothing that we can do except be present, pray, pass out tissues, and share our sympathy. As I have often quoted the line in this course, grief is messy. And it seems more so when children are involved.

## CHAPTER 13

# SUICIDE

## WHAT DOES THE BIBLE AND THE CHURCH SAY ABOUT SUICIDE?

To be honest, we are flying blind on this subject. In all of the stories that are recorded in the metanarrative of our religion, there are only six stories that resemble a form of suicide, and only half of them are significant. The one that we are most familiar with is the death of Judas, who apparently succumbs to guilt following his betrayal of Jesus (Matthew 27:3-10). The second major suicide attempt is the death of Saul, when he instructs his armor-bearer to ready his sword so that he may fall on it (1 Samuel 31:1-6). The most in-depth narrative (and one that is more redemptive in nature) is the end to the tragic story of Samson. After being captured and tortured by the Philistines, Samson prays for one final bout of strength so that he may bring God's judgment against Israel's foes. Paraded for sport, Samson literally brings down the house as he pushes two columns apart in the Temple of Dagon, causing a collapse of the building (Judges 16:23-31).

Yet, despite the present-day squeamish attitude toward suicide, the Bible says little about the self-taking of life. As William Phipps writes, "The biblical writers neither condemn nor commend those whom they record as having taken their own lives. Perhaps the narrators thought it was fitting for Samson, Saul and Judas to respond to their varied situations by committing suicide."[116] These stories are part of the narrative that defines our religion, thus suicide, whether positively or negatively, becomes a practice of our religion. What is more confounding

---

[116] William E. Phipps, "Christian Perspective on Suicide," *The Christian Century* 102 (30 October 1985): 970.

is that this issue is rarely discussed by theologians, biblical scholars, ethicists, or ministers. In fact, a review of my own library revealed the following:

- Out of half a dozen or so introductory textbooks on theology, I was only able to find two references to suicide. First, Bradley Hanson, *in a footnote*, reminds us that those who commit suicide "usually suffers from deep depression in which the body's chemical balance is severely disturbed and does not freely choose suicide."[117] Second, Millard Erickson provides an evaluation of Thomas Altizer's liberal "Death of God" theological construct (a.k.a., secular theology) in which Altizer equates the Crucifixion to a successful suicide attempt by the God of the Old Testament.[118]

- In terms of books on Christian ethics and morality, only Dietrich Bonhoeffer offers this perspective: "God has reserved to himself the right to determine the end of life, because he alone knows the goal to which it is his will to lead it. . . .Even if a person's earthly life has become a torment for him, he must commit it intact to God's hand, from which it came."[119]

- And, when reviewing my vast amount of treatises on pastoral theology, I found only passing references to suicide, such as in Thomas Oden's book where he adds "juvenile suicide statistics" into a list of weapons used by "modern hedonists" who attempt to promote narcissism over Christian spirituality.[120] And the references to suicide in pastoral counseling textbooks offer an approach for how to minister in such situations but offer little in terms of theology, philosophy, or psychology.

So how are we to understand suicide from a theological perspective? First of all, we must erase some of the mysticism regarding suicide. It is,

---

[117] Bradley C. Hanson, *Introduction to Christian Theology* (Minneapolis: Fortress, 1997), 15, n. 6.

[118] Millard J. Erickson, *Christian Theology*, 2nd ed. (Grand Rapids, MI: Baker Academic, 1998), 126.

[119] Dietrich Bonhoeffer, *Ethics* (New York: Macmillan, 1955), 124-125.

[120] Thomas C. Oden, *Pastoral Theology: Essentials for Ministry* (New York: HarperCollins, 1983), 212.

after all, simply another form of death. The only difference is that it is by our own hand instead of at the hand of another or by natural powers. Thus, it is possible that we may apply the sixth command to suicide: "You shall not murder" (Exodus 20:13). Terence Fretheim favors the traditional KJV translation of "kill" because it "serves the community of faith best" in that it reminds us "that all life belongs to God," thus echoing Bonhoeffer's above statement.[121] If we understand suicide as a form of killing (which it is difficult not to) then suicide certainly falls under this command.

In addition to this passage, there are also the matching passages in 1 Corinthians regarding our bodies being "God's temple." First in chapter 3, Paul writes:

> Do you not know that you are a temple of God and that the Spirit of God dwells in you? If any man destroys the temple of God, God will destroy him, for the temple of God is holy, and that is what you are (3:16-17).

And, then, in chapter 6, he writes:

> Or do you not know that your body is a temple of the Holy Spirit who is in you, whom you have from God, and that you are not your own? For you have been bought with a price: therefore glorify God in your body (6:19-20).

In both passages, Paul is exhorting the Corinthians Christians, people well-associated with the vice of lust, to remember that they are now the Temple that God resides in. Thus, that Temple is to remain unspoiled so that God may continually dwell within them. In a way, then, to cut down our own lives would be to knock down part of that wall. However, we must also admit that the Bible is specific regarding our appointment with death. As the Preacher says, there is "A time to give birth and a time to die" (Ecclesiastes 3:2a), and the anonymous author of Hebrews reminds us that "it is appointed for men to die once" (Hebrews 9:27). Thus, with these passages in mind, it is crucial that we

---

[121] Terence E. Fretheim, *Exodus*, Interpretation: A Bible Commentary for Teaching and Preaching (Louisville: John Knox Press, 1981), 233.

not discount suicide as the avenue by which some cross from this life to the next. For to some, taking their own life is more than dying on their own terms—it is keeping their appointment with death. In any way, coming to a conclusion regarding suicide is an exercise in operational theology—the set of doctrine that we use to guide our lives.

## THE REALITY OF SUICIDE

Seneca once wrote that "death lies near at hand. . . .Whether the throat is strangled by a knot, or water stops the breathing, or the hard ground crushes in the skull of one falling headlong to its surface, or flame inhaled cuts off the course of respiration—be it what it may; the end is swift." Noted psychiatrist and author Kay Redfield Jamison writes,

> We may never know who or why or how the first to kill himself did (or herself; we may never know that either). But it is very likely that once suicide occurred and others were cognizant of it, the act was repeated—in part because the reasons and means would remain integral to the psychological and physical environment, and in part because animals and humans learn, to considerable extent, through imitation. Suicide, dangerously, has a contagious aspect; it has, as well, for the vulnerable, an indisputable appeal as the solution of last resort.[122]

Jamison is certainly an expert on the subject of suicide, struggling herself for many years with bipolar disorder and multiple contemplations regarding taking her own life.[123]

> Suicide is a particularly awful way to die: the mental suffering leading up to it is usually prolonged, intense, and unpalliated. There is no morphine equivalent to ease

---

[122] Kay Redfield Jamison, *Night Falls Fast: Understanding Suicide* (New York: Vintage Books, 1999), 12.

[123] See her *An Unquiet Mind: A Memoir of Moods and Madness* (New York: Vintage Books), 1997. She has also written a compelling study that connects bipolar disorder with "the artistic temperament"; see *Touched by Fire: Manic-Depressive Illness and the Artistic Temperament* (New York: Free Press, 1996).

the acute pain, and death not uncommonly is violent and grisly. The suffering of the suicidal is private and inexpressible, leaving family members, friends, and colleagues to deal with an almost unfathomable kind of loss, as well as guilt. Suicide carries in its aftermath a level of confusion and devastation that is, for the most part, beyond description.[124]

Without a doubt, suicide, especially when successful, is a crisis that many will deal with and few are prepared for. According to the National Institute for Mental Health and the Center of Disease Control and Prevention, suicide was the tenth major cause of death among Americans in 2007, accounting for over 35,000 deaths.[125] Yet, dealing with the death of someone is tricky and extremely difficult to prepare for. In my experience, no suicide has even gone the same way. Some who were unsuccessful were repentant of their actions and some acted as if nothing had happened. In the cases of those who were successful, some families wailed loudly over their loved ones while others simply walked away.

## MINISTRY IN SUICIDE

I have had very few encounters with people contemplating suicide. Usually if they actually bring themselves (or allow themselves to be brought) to the Emergency Room, then they are really serious about taking their lives. They are, however, aware that they need help. My experience primarily comes through ministering to families who are confronted with the grisly reality that a loved one violently removed himself or herself from this world. And, as with most ministry in times of death, there is really little that can be done except pray and offer a shoulder to cry on.

However, to not share some of my experiences would be unfair. What I offer is nothing grand or refined; simply my experiences. First, be ready to listen to those who are thinking about or have actually

---

[124] Jamison, *Night Falls Fast: Understanding Suicide*, 24.

[125] www.nimh.nih.gov/health/publications/suicide-in-the-us-statistics-and-prevention/index.shtml; accessed 14 November 2010.

attempted suicide. During my clinical training, I was called early one morning to the Emergency Room to speak with a middle-aged man who said that he was suicidal. As we talked, I learned that he was a loner and was in a menial job. His parents had died a few years before and he had not been able to maintain a stable marriage because of his struggle with homosexuality. He said that he actually had no means to take his own life, yet it was something that he had been thinking about. (Now, it is important to remember that if someone is seriously thinking about suicide, they will find a way to act out their plan.) After we talked for some time, he asked me to pray for him. He was later released.

Secondly, take seriously those people who have created a plan. One of the intriguing aspects of suicide is the psychological disconnect that is involved. Many professionals will say that those who contemplate suicide have suffered a "mental break" because of the plot that they are conspiring. Yet, there is a great deal of mental strength and capacity that goes into planning a suicide. If the plan is vague and generic, then there may not be as much cause for concern. Although the threat should be honored, it does not require the extreme intervention that a carefully conceived plan requires. As Howard Stone instructs,

> If a person has a very specific plan, has spent time thinking in detail about how to commit the act, has selected a lethal method, and has the means readily available, *the risk of suicide is very serious and requires immediate action* on the part of the intervener.[126]

In one case, I was counseling a young woman who was intent on killing herself in order to get even with her mother. I quickly realized that I was talking with an intelligent albeit misguided young woman. When I realized that talking was not productive, I employed a play therapy technique. I asked the young woman to draw some pictures for me—how she felt at the moment; how she felt about being in the hospital; how she felt at home; what she would do if she went home. The final picture was telling—she drew, in detail, how she would successfully take her life through a second attempt. As a result, the attending physician and

---

[126] Howard W. Stone, *Crisis Counseling*, 3rd ed., Creative Pastoral Care and Counseling Series (Minneapolis: Fortress Press, 2009), 60.

I agreed that she needed to be committed to a local psychiatric facility. Unless you are a licensed physician or psychiatrist, you do not have the authority to commit someone, although you most certainly have the authority to intervene in their situation and get them the medical or psychological attention they require.

Third, be ready to discuss religious and spiritual concerns with those who are contemplating suicide. On one Sunday morning, I was called to the Emergency Room for another situation, only to discover that a middle-aged woman had been brought in earlier due to a suicide attempt. She had swallowed a large number of pills and had to have her stomach flushed and be intubated in order to keep her airway from closing up. As was the protocol at that facility, a consult for a suicide assessment was sent through for this patient. I went and visited her later in the day. She was repentant for what she had done and realized that God had spared her life through the medical intervention. She asked me if I thought she would have gone to hell had she succeeded and if I thought she could be forgiven of this act. I told her that I was not in the place to pass judgment on anyone's eternal destination except my own. However, I also told her that I was confident that she could be forgiven of any sin she may have engaged in. After praying for her, I recommended that she contact our counseling center for a follow-up appointment.

Fourth, be prepared to minister to families when suicides are successful. On another Sunday morning, I was called to the Emergency Room for a cardiac arrest caused by a drug overdose. The patient was a beautiful, college student who, according to her family, had a great future ahead of her, yet she chose a path riddled with prostitution and drugs. When the family was able to view the body, there were numerous questions with no available answers. There were tears that flowed openly, and all I could do was provide them with tissues to wipe those tears away. Even my prayer seemed paltry in comparison to the situation. Yet, as I have said all along, presence is more important than action.

There is one technical concern that I should mention here. If a patient comes to the hospital and dies as a result of a suicide, the local coroner will be contacted. In almost every case, an autopsy will be required, especially if the patient is young. This is important to know—and to ask when you are with the family—because the hospital will not release the body to the funeral home; it will go to the state coroner's office. Following the autopsy, the body will be released to the funeral home of the family's choice. A word of caution is necessary here: following an autopsy, a person's body is fairly mutilated. A friend of mine who operated a funeral home and another who was a fellow chaplain who did make-up for burial preparation have both said that it is extremely difficult to make bodies presentable following an autopsy. This is something for you to consider when ministering to families following such a death.

CHAPTER 14

# ETHICAL SITUATIONS[127]

"What do I do?" Typically, this question comes from patients and family members who faced with the gut-wrenching decision of what to do regarding treatment. However, on one particular evening, this question was posed to me by a young medical resident who was faced with guiding a family through making one of the most painful decisions of their lives. She and I discussed the patient's condition and the family's concerns related to keeping the patient on the ventilator or discontinuing aggressive medical treatment and placing the patient on "comfort measures." After several moments of discussing the options among ourselves, she asked, "Will you speak to the family for me? I overheard you praying with them earlier, so I know that they respect and trust you." I composed myself and entered into the arena of ethics—to choose pain or to choose salvation. I am neither a professional ethicist nor a regular member of an ethics committee. What I am is a minister who serves as the presence of God in moments of crisis, one who has chosen to stand in the gap between hurting people and the magic that confuses even the most educated of men. What I offer in this chapter is nothing new or profound. I only offer a reminder that we who practice the sacred arts are more than just a pebble that balances the scale—we are the ones holding the balance between chaos and justice.

## THE ROLE OF RELIGION IN MEDICINE

What is the role of religion in medicine? Are there not two more conceptually confusing terms in our shared language? For most of the

---

[127] A portion of this article appeared as an essay entitled "The Role of Ministers in Medical Ethics," *Restoration Quarterly* 53, number 2 (2011): 96-100.

duration of human existence, religion and medicine were seen as the same thing. For example, in ancient Greece, the sick and suffering would travel to the Temple of Asclepius at Epidaurus, in order to offer prayers to the god through clay sculptures of what ailed them. The Greeks believed that Asclepius would hear their prayers and send healing through the work of the priests who worked in the temple. I remember being amazed at the vast number of hands, feet, eyes, and other diseased appendages that littered the storage rooms at the museum. And while it may sound silly to our modern, illuminated ears, what is religion other than "a system of beliefs and practices that provides values to give life meaning and coherence by directing a person towards transcendence"?[128] In times of distress, the Greeks called upon their gods for solace. Are we really any different? As Verna Benner Carson and Harold Koenig remind us,

> According to multiple surveys, the majority of Americans believe in the power of God or prayer to improve the course of an illness. As healthcare professionals, we must be sensitive to the power of these beliefs to influence views and decisions regarding issues such as end-of-life care, suicide, stem cell research, euthanasia, rationing of healthcare, and abortion.[129]

People are looking for direction, for a compass that will guide them through the journey of life. For many, religion is that compass, that guide that helps them make sense of life. Darryl Macer argues that "most people find religion to be a much more important source of guidance in life than science. Any theory of bioethics that will be applied to peoples of the world must be acceptable to the common trends of major religious thought." And as Gary Batchelor reminds us, people are not looking for a cleverly contrived diagnosis for what is wrong with them—they are looking for relief from their pain, relief that they often find through prayer, ritual, and guidance.[130] Yet, even people who are

---

[128] Winfried Corduan, *Neighboring Faiths: A Christian Introduction to World Religions* (Downers Grove, IL: InterVarsity Press, 1998), 21.

[129] Verna Benner Carson and Harold G. Koenig, *Spiritual Caregiving: Healthcare as a Ministry* (Philadelphia/London: Templeton Foundation, 2004), 85.

[130] Gary Batchelor, "Spirituality and Clinical Ethics: Inseparably Intertwined," *Healing Spirit* 4 (Spring 2009): 16-17.

guided by religion, as my family was when my grandfather was battling in his final days with lung cancer, must, at times, answer the question of "What should I do." As practitioners of the sacred arts, we must be ready to answer the question and provide the necessary guidance. It is to these tasks that we now turn.

# THREE ETHICAL QUESTIONS

In answering the question, "What do I do?" there are three issues that must be considered.[131] First, there is the question of *what will be done.* In this question, we, the practitioners, are asking how we and the family members will solve the specific dilemma that we find ourselves in. Second, there is the question of *what can be done.* In this question, we are looking over all of the available options that have been approved to determine which ones fit which situations. Finally, there is the question of *what should be done.* In this question, we are dealing with the areas of public policy and social justice. Madison Powers and Ruth Faden say that the area of social justice is most important because in striving to maintain our humanity we will come to the ethical decision that is needed in the situations we face.[132] This is probably the most difficult question to answer because it is in answering this question that we often find ourselves in moral and ethical quandaries. In my experience, the story usually works something like this: A patient is brought to the hospital in some form of distress. The medical team performs their examinations and assessments and comes to a conclusion about which course of action to take. In a discussion with the family, the physicians present their plan to the family, and the family rejects the plan. This creates the quandary because the patient's life, wellbeing, and dignity hang in the balance. Sometimes the situation is resolved and the patient's situation is relieved, and sometimes the situation goes round and round while the patient suffers. As the ones who represent the spiritual dimension of

[131] Laurel Arthur Burton and Donald F. Phillips, "The Role of Chaplains in Ethical Decision Making," in *Chaplaincy Services in Contemporary Health Care,* ed. Laurel Arthur Burton (Schaumberg, IL: College of Chaplains, Inc., 1992), 43.
[132] Madison Powers and Ruth Faden, *Social Justice: The Moral Foundations of Public Health and Health Policy,* Issues in Biomedical Ethics (Oxford/New York: Oxford University Press, 2008), 6-7.

healthcare, how do ministers enter into ethical discussions in order to provide holistic care to patients and family members who are suffering?

## THREE APPROACHES TO ETHICAL DECISIONS

Dealing with ethical issues on a personal level is difficult enough as it is. How can we possibly expect ourselves to do the correct thing every time when there are unnumbered positive and negative consequences to every action? Yet, as people of faith, we are called to live lives that are "holy and blameless and beyond reproach" before God (Colossians 1:23). Hauerwas and Willimon remind us that ethics, in a religious sense, is not a category of academic inquiry that can be studied and sorted into a fancy bullet-point list; it is a way of life that guides us and shapes us into becoming morally mature beings.[133] Yet, how do we go about making ethical decisions that are morally and practically-appropriate?

It is generally accepted that the practice of ethics can be summed up as "rules," "relativism," or "relationships."[134] The "rules" approach tells us that there are guidelines and regulations for a reason. According to Burton and Phillips, "The belief is that some things are right and other things are wrong in and of themselves, independent of their consequences."[135] In the context of medical ethics, the "rules" approach says that there are some interventions that are always correct (i.e., administering the appropriate dose of morphine to relieve a patient's pain yet not cause them to go comatose), and there are some interventions that are always incorrect (i.e., performing CPR on a patient with a "Do Not Resuscitate" order who is coding). In this situation, the minister, as resident religious specialist, functions as a moral advisor and, if need be, moral enforcer, what is often referred to as the "priestly" role.

The "relativism" approach encourages us to do whatever feels right in that moment. Again Burton and Phillips write, "The basic truth here is that there is no overriding truth, and therefore, people should be

---

[133] Stanley Hauerwas and William H. Willimon, *Resident Aliens: Life in the Christian Colony* (Nashville: Abingdon, 1989), 69-72.

[134] Burton and Phillips, "The Role of Chaplains in Ethical Decision Making," 44-46; see also, James Kellenberger, *Moral Relativism, Moral Diversity, and Human Relationships* (University Park, PA: The Pennsylvania State University, 2001); and Peter Singer, *Ethics*, Oxford Readers Series (Oxford: Oxford University Press, 1994).

[135] Ibid., 44.

free to decide what fits their own situation and have the power to make their own choices."[136] In the context of medical ethics, the "relativism" approach says that patients (or family members, if patients cannot speak for themselves) are free to choose whatever they want. The most apt illustration in recent time would be the work of Jack Kevorkian, the physician who promised to perform euthanasia on any patient for any reason. Whether it be abortion as a form of birth control, the use of marijuana for pain management, refusing physical therapy, or electing to have cosmetic surgeries against a physician's advice, the "relativism" approach says that patient's should be free to care for themselves, no matter how destructive their actions may be. In this situation, the minister functions as an "advocate" for the patient so that his or her rights and concerns are expressed and heard.

The "relationship" approach encourages us to build healthy avenues of communication between patients, family members, and the medical staff in order to facilitate conflict that arises over disagreements in a patient's treatment. In short, the "relationship" approach says, "Let's talk about it." This approach is inductive, where "one might find an emphasis on virtue along with the necessity of listening to the narratives produced by the participants."[137] In the context of medical ethics, the "relationship" approach seeks to hear the stories that have brought the participants to this point in the patient's life. As they share their stories and experiences, patients, family members, and medical personal are able to develop an understanding of one another, to bridge cultural differences that may be causing the ethical dilemma.[138] In this situation, the minister functions as a "negotiator," working to create sacred space so that a covenant of care can be established.

## DIMENSIONS OF THE MINISTER'S ROLE

Although each approach has its strengths and limitations, each approach is appropriate in its own way. Thus, the final area is not to select one of the approaches to use over the other two, but to understand our place

---

[136] Ibid., 45.

[137] Ibid.

[138] A useful text for further reflection in this area would be, Michelle LeBaron, *Bridging Cultural Conflicts: A New Approach for a Changing World* (San Francisco: Jossey-Bass/ John Wiley and Sons, Inc., 2003).

in each approach. Ethics is a tricky game to play with only one set of cards, thus we must be prepared to play with multiple decks, even playing in multiple games at once. Therefore, our task is to understand the dimensions of our role in ethical decisions.

In an influential article, Don Browning notes five "dimensions" of the minister's role in ethical decision-making.[139] I believe his applications can also be applied to the minister for the congregational setting. First, the minister is a *servant of health*. We serve the needs of the patients and the community. Part of that ministry includes serving viable institutions within our communities. How do we do this? We offer prayer, sacred readings, rituals, and our spiritual insight in order to bring emotional and spiritual healing. Second, the minister is a *cultural anthropologist*. We shape an understanding of health according to the worldviews that are presented to us. Our role is often to decipher the worldview codes that we hear during conversations and map that worldview in our minds so that we can translate it to the other party. Third, the minister is a *negotiator of worldviews*. We provide a new voice for differences. As we are mapping these differing worldviews, we stand between them and translate what each side is saying to the other. We do this in order to build mutual trust and respect for one another. Fourth, the minister is a *stimulator of ethical deliberation*. We ask the questions that need to be asked, not conduct the actual consultation. And finally, the minister is a *stimulator of spiritual growth*. We guide patients, family members, and medical staff in reflecting on their values in the midst of suffering and crisis in order to lead them to a "holy ground" experience. For it is in this "holy ground" experience that clarity, purpose, and reconciliation are revealed to those who are party to the ethical dilemma.

As we come to the conclusion of this matter, we accept the fact that much more could have been said and, perhaps, much more should have been said. Yet, ministry in the hospital requires little evolution to remain relevant. As my clinical supervisor often reminded my peer group, all we have is ourselves when we enter into a spiritual conversation with someone in need. All we need to do is accept our role as servant, shepherd, and, sometimes, stimulator of ethical deliberations.

---

[139] Don S. Browning, "Hospital Chaplaincy as Public Ministry," *Second Opinion* 1 (1986): 66-75.

## ADVANCED DIRECTIVES AND OTHER DOCUMENTS

"What exactly is an 'advanced directive' and what exactly do they do?" I am not sure how many times I was asked this question. According to Junkerman and Schiedermayer, "An advanced directive (AD) is a statement a patient makes, while still in possession of decision-making capacity, about how treatment decisions should be made at some time in the future if he or she loses the capacity to make such decisions."[140] And it is the "still in possession of decision-making capacity" that is important. During my residency, I was often called upon to witness the signing of advanced directives. (Needless to say, a pediatric chaplain does not complete many of these things.) For example, I was called by one of my peers to witness one as our office manager notarized it. When I arrived at the room, the patient was going through his address book to make sure that the addresses that he was going to use were correct. As he began filling out the form, he suddenly changed his mind. This would mean that we would have start over with a brand new form. On the second attempt, he filled out a name, then asked if a phone number would be required. When he was informed that it would be helpful because the physicians cannot mail their questions, the man replied, "Well, that's going to be difficult because she died a few years ago." (I'll take a moment for this to sink in.) He said this with a straight face, with all the seriousness he could muster. Yet, we were required to honor his signature because he had not been deemed medically incompetent by a physician, even though everyone that had cared for him knew that he was.

Only a licensed physician (medical or psychiatric) can declare someone medically incompetent. Unless this is done, anyone wishing to complete an advanced directive has the legal right to do so. In fact, I highly encourage you to complete your own, appointing your own advocates and discussing with them your wishes regarding your medical care in case you are ever unable to speak for yourself. There are three types of advanced directives:

---

[140] Charles Junkerman and David Schiedermayer, *Practical Ethics for Students, Interns, and Residents: A Short Reference Manual* (Frederick, MD: University Publishing Group, Inc., 1994), 46. This volume is now in its third edition, published in 2008.

- *Living Will*—A "living will" states that a patient desires to die as naturally as possible and not be kept alive by invasive forms of treatments and therapy.
- *Medical Power of Attorney (MPOA)*—A "medical power of attorney" states who may make medical decisions for the patient if he or she is unable to do so. The important point of contention here is that the decisions are to be what the *patient* would want, not what the family member or friend would want. Whereas a "living will" is fairly cut-and-dry as to its stipulations and limitations, a MPOA allows a patient more freedom to chose what treatments or interventions can be used.
- *Combined Living Will/Medical Power of Attorney*—As the name implies, this form is a combination of the two. Most states are offering this form now.

In addition, there are also two others types of forms that ministers should be aware of. First, there is the "DNR," or "Do Not Resuscitate" form. This form indicates that a patient, if found in unconscious, unresponsive, or in some form of respiratory or cardiac arrest, asks that medical intervention not be used to revive her or him. In essence, the patient is asking to be allowed to die. These forms are usually included in with a patient's "living will" as an added assurance that his or her wishes will be carried out. Once the patient's chart is tagged as a "DNR," it is a major medical violation to attempt CPR, intubation, or any other form of invasive intervention on such a patient. Second, there is the "medical surrogate" form. In this form, a physician appoints a family member to make medical decisions for a patient who did not prepare any advanced directives. A "medical surrogate" form functions exactly like a "medical power of attorney," although it expires following the patient's discharge, death, or regaining of decision-making ability.

It is important to realize that, while advanced directives are very important, they are of little use in a crisis situation. EMTs and emergency room staff are training to do one thing—save lives. Notr this example: A patient collapses at home and becomes unresponsive. A concerned family member calls 911 and reports the emergency. The ambulance arrives and the crew starts performing CPR. All the while that this is going on, the patient's "living will" sits with instructions to let him pass from this life in such a situation. Yet, the family member does not think about this, reacting to the situation out of a fear of losing their loved one. The crew loads the patient into the ambulance and takes him to the nearest emergency room. There, the ER staff continues treating the patient aggressively, intubating the patient and beginning several medications. Eventually, the patient is transferred to the ICU, where the same form of treatment is continued. However, the patient's family arrives at the hospital to discover this situation. When the attending physician speaks with the family about what has been done, the family is astonished because they were aware of the patient's wishes to be allowed to die in such a situation. Shocked by the family's news, the physician must decide whether to defer to the patient's wishes or continue treating the patient as he or she has been doing so. And I can tell you from personal experience, physicians and family members—when faced with this situation—often *do not* honor the wishes of their loved one, often pushing the patient's body and the medical team well beyond their intended limits. As ministers and pastoral caregivers, we must remember that the dignity of the patient is, in the moment of crisis, our primary concern. Thus, as we discussed above, we are often called upon to be the "moral enforcer" of justice in the technological culture.

I know that this chapter does not offer nearly enough to prepare you for an extensive career in dealing with medical ethics. That was not the intention; the intention was simply to introduce you to the reality that sometimes you will be required to help families make very difficult decisions. For more information on the various aspects of medical ethics, advanced directives, invasive interventions, and the discontinuation of them, I would recommend the following books:

- Hank Dunn, *Hard Choices for Living People: CPR, Artificial Feeding, Comfort Care, and the Patient with a Life-Threatening Illness*, 5th ed. (Herndon, VA: A & A Publishers, Inc., 2009).
- Tony Hope, *Medical Ethics: A Very Short Introduction*, Very Short Introduction Series (New York/Oxford: Oxford University Press, 2004).
- Albert Jonsen, Mark Siegler, and William Winslade, *Clinical Ethics: A Practical Approach to Ethical Decisions in Clinical Medicine*, 7th ed. (New York: McGraw-Hill Medical, 2010).

- Junkerman and Schiedermayer, *Practical Ethics for Students, Interns, and Residents: A Short Reference Manual* (see n. 14 for full reference).
- William Molloy and Virginia Mepham, *Let Me Decide: The Health Care Directive that Speaks for You When You Can't* (New York: Penguin Books, 1992).
- Thomas A. Shannon and Charles N. Faso, *Let Them Go Free: A Guide to Withdrawing Life Support* (Washington, DC: Georgetown University Press, 2007).

# CHAPTER 15

# MARRIAGE AND FAMILY ISSUES

In most books on pastoral care or crisis ministry, the subject of marriage and family crises would not typically be touched. These topics would typically be reserved for a course in counseling or family ministry. The reason for this is because this subject is difficult to define. During my clinical training, the family issues were discussed only within the contexts of personality theory, co-dependency, and dysfunctional relationships. Also, I should be honest that I do not have a great deal of experience with marriage and family crises, since most of my congregational ministry experience has been with smaller, rural-based congregations. However, I do feel that this topic, based on my *hospital* experience, is important. Thus, what I offer is a brief introduction and summary of some pressing issues that relate to families in our technology-driven, emotionally-withdrawn society.

## DIVORCE

For most ministers, divorce is the one family-based crisis that we will come into contact with. It is a commonly-accepted aspect of our society. Growing up in Nashville in a congregation of 700, there was only one couple where one spouse had been married previously. In another congregation that I was part of (a congregation of about 250), I can think at least a half of dozen couples where at least one spouse had been married before.

Ministry in times of divorce is difficult because one spouse usually does not see the divorce coming. It is a surprise to them when their spouse hands them the filed injunction. And, to be brutally honest, there is little that can be done to salvage a marriage once it comes to this point. Yet, since we are in community with those who are experiencing divorce, our ministry is to be to both parties.

## PHYSICAL AND SEXUAL ABUSE

It is no secret that physical violence within the family is at "epidemic" rates.[141] In past time, it was always husbands abusing wives. There is this classic scene in *L.A. Confidential* (1997) where beat cop Russell Crowe and his slightly inebriated partner are patrolling the quiet streets of suburban Los Angeles on Christmas Eve. They come across a house where a husband is physically assaulting his wife. Crowe jumps out of his car, bursts into the house, and begins returning the husband's actions in kind. He drags the man outside the house and throws him to the ground. He takes the husband's wallet, pulls the cash out of it, and gives it to the wife, telling her to leave her husband. He then threatens the husband with arresting him on a "kiddie raper" charge if he tries to harm his wife again. It is an archetypal scene about manhood—the drunk husband beats his wife for no apparent reason other than he simply can, and the policeman with a "Messiah complex" defends a beaten wife for no apparent reason. As Clinebell writes,

> In other words, violence against women is a consequence of the unequal distribution of social status and of economic, political, and legal power between women and men. It is also the consequence of the learned powerlessness and passivity that many women feel when they relate to men. Furthermore, it is the result of the fact that most men, in patriarchal cultures, learn to define women as "other" and to feel masculine only to the degree that they are different from women.[142]

Yet, it should be noted that spousal abuse is not only directed against women, but also can be directed *by* women. Originally, it was thought that "husband battering" was a reaction to abuse that wives endured. However, according to the websites EndDomesticAbuse.com and Fact. On.ca, abuse by wives against husbands is becoming more and more common, and more and more gruesome.

---

[141] Howard Clinebell, *Basic Types of Pastoral Care and Counseling: Resources for the Ministry of Healing and Growth*, rev. ed. (Nashville: Abingdon, 1984), 305.
[142] Ibid., 305-306.

When we become aware of an abusive situation, we should intervene as quickly as possible. Here are some guidelines to consider when minister to people in abusive relationships:

- If the violence is chronic and the abuser is unmotivated to seek help, then the spouse should seek to find safe lodging for himself or herself and any children. In the case of child abuse where the parents are or may be at fault, it is imperative to seek medical attention for the child. Hospitals, in the case of abuse, will assume protective custody of the child until CPS rules on the situation.
- Ministers should assist the abusive spouse in finding recovery services that can provide counseling and direction.
- Providing marriage counseling may be appropriate and effective in cases where the violence is more infrequent. However, the minister must be cautious not to enter into a potentially dangerous situation where the outbursts are acute.
- Victims of abuse must "unlearn what they have learned" when it comes to living in abusive relationships. Most spouses who live in abusive relationships have co-dependent personalities. They must be made aware of this and the tendencies that go along with it.

It is also important that victims of abuse and rape seek medical attention immediately. All too often, especially in cases of rape, women wait until it is too late for any intervention to be useful. It is also important for victims of sexual abuse to seek counseling and to become part of a support group for continued encouragement. It is even more important for children who are the victims of sexual abuse to receive counseling. From my experience working with children who have been sexually abused, they often become abusers themselves.

## LOSING A JOB

Our country has learned the hard way how to survive during lean economic times. From a surplus of bankruptcies to bulging unemployment lines to rampant home foreclosures, our country has really suffered the last few years. As someone who has lost a job (or two), I can tell you that there really is no difference between being fired and being laid off; one just sounds nicer than the other. Whether you are young and just starting out or older and thinking more about retirement than starting over again, losing a job is an extremely stressful crisis. From my own experience, here are some suggestions on how to help those experiencing this type of crisis:

- Work with your congregation's benevolence program or local food pantry to provide food for the family. Although the family may qualify for food stamps or an Electronic Balance Transfer (EBT) card, it could take a couple of weeks for this process to get started.
- Direct the spouse who lost his or her job to the local unemployment office. Unemployment benefits are not much; however they can be helpful in paying bills and working with agencies in seeking relief from the burden of stretching thin money.
- Contact the local Community Action Organization. This organization works with energy suppliers (gas and electric) to develop payment plans for families that are struggling financially. Most utility companies are willing to set up an income-based payment plan so that the energy sources do not have to be turned off. However, they are stringent, and paying on time is mandatory.
- In addition to applying for unemployment benefits, the person who has lost a job should be connected with either a workforce program that is designed to help people find employment (e.g., a temp agency) or a career center where they can learn new skills that may lead them to a more new career (or at least a new job). In some cases, especially in cases where the loss of the job affects the person psychologically, counseling may be needed in order to guide the person through accepting the situation and moving on in a new direction.

One thing people who lose a job will need is continued encouragement and prayer. Looking for a job is difficult enough. It is even more difficult when you are coming out of a failed employment situation because employers are less likely to hire fired candidates. While it is often a good idea to pass along job possibilities to those looking, it is best to only do so if there is a guarantee for hire. If not and the person is not hired, it only added to their frustration, disappointment, and depression. Also, do not offer opportunities unless you think that the person and the job match well. To do otherwise could jeopardize your situation if you recommend the person for the position.

## COMMUNITY DISASTERS

Several years ago, an apartment complex in Huntington, West Virginia, caught fire and the entire building burned. There were some fatalities, although there were far more injured survivors. Cabell Huntington Hospital, being the only burn center in the area, received all of the victims from the fire. I was not yet working at Cabell, but the situation did become a case study the next year from my peer group concerning ministering in a community disaster. My supervisor's advice was simple: "Walk around and look like you know what you're doing. That way, no one panics more than they need to." To be honest, it's good advice, given the situation.

Most communities have crisis response teams that are staffed with religious and psychological professionals. Being on such a team requires specialized training in emergency management, which you can usually receive in a graduate course on crisis intervention or emergency management. Also, the Red Cross (www.redcross.org) and the Federal Emergency Management Agency (www.fema.gov) provide training to concerned professionals who want to be ready for such disasters.

# Pastoral Care Note

Patient Visited: _____

Location: _____

Date/Time: _____

Age: _____    Gender: _____

Marital Status: _____

Ethnicity: _____

Number of Visit(s): _____

Reason for Visit: _____
_____
_____
_____

Condition of Patient: _____
_____
_____
_____

Reactions/Responses/Comments from Patient:


Condition of Family (if present):


Reactions/Responses/Comments from Family (if present):


Actions Taken by Minister:


Reflection on the Visit:


Follow-Up/Referral Notes (if necessary):